THE CHURCH MUSICIAN

THE CHURCH MUSICIAN
REVISED EDITION

PAUL WESTERMEYER

Augsburg Fortress
Minneapolis

THE CHURCH MUSICIAN
Revised Edition

Original hardcover edition, *The Church Musician*, published by Harper & Row, copyright © 1988.

Editor: Norma Aamodt-Nelson
Production editor: Lani Willis
Interior design: Linda Parriott
Cover art: Andrew Powell
Cover design: David Meyer

Library of Congress Cataloging-in Publication Data
Westermeyer, Paul, 1940-
    The church musician / Paul Westermeyer. —Rev. Ed.
        p.   cm.
    Includes bibliographical references (p.) and index.
    ISBN 0-8066-3399-9
    1. Church music—Handbooks, manuals, etc. 2. Music in churches.
3. Ministers of music.   I. Title.
ML3001.W5   1997
264'.2—dc21   97-11149
                                                              CIP
                                                              MN

The paper used in this publication meets the minimum requirements of American National Standard for Information Science—Permanence of Paper for Printed Library Materials, ANSI Z329.48-1984.   ™
                                                              ∞

Manufactured in the U.S.A   ISBN 0-8066-3399-9   10-33999
            05   5 6 7 8 9

To
the congregations,
worshiping communities,
and choirs
with whom I have been privileged
to sing the story

Table of Contents

Foreword

PICTURE THE YEAR 1998, the tenth anniversary of this book. The publisher presents it in a third revised edition and with a new title: *The Christian Cantor.* I can dream. I can dream, first, that there may be a long life for the book, that there might be many editions, some revisions. I can also dream that by then Paul Westermeyer will have made his point so effectively that the book can bear the new title.

The Christian Cantor might well have been the title of the first edition. Chapter Two tells why, and I do not want to rob the plot of any of its suspense. No master of suspense, however, can keep from the reader a notion of why the word *cantor* is not in the title . . . yet. The author, publisher, and booksellers all know that in our culture, most people associate the term *cantor* with the synagogue. They might not yet connect it as well with the person who leads "the people's song" in Christian worship.

The Jewish roots of the term not only do not disturb Paul Westermeyer, they please him. He reminds us that Christian worship has learned much from the synagogue and must return to its roots there for refreshment. In the modern world, however, the Christian public knows the synagogue cantor not through acquaintance with the cantor at the friendly temple down the block. No, according to the author, the role model is "the great voice like Robert Merrill, Richard Tucker, or Jan Peerce," the voice of people who developed from the Jewish cantorial tradition to become opera stars. They are or were indeed great men with great voices, but they will not do as models for the "leader of the people's song." They are essentially performers. Performers are not what this book has in mind.

Westermeyer hopes that bit by bit, year by year, more and more Christian congregations will learn to think of their musical leaders not as performers—though their standards of performance, he argues, must be of the highest—but as participant leaders. The key term has to do with what they lead: *the people's song*. That role is so obvious one hardly needs a book about it and yet, in reality, it is so overlooked that one could use a shelf full of books to compensate for its neglect.

There is a radical notion tucked away in the apparently innocuous idea of the people's song. Not many congregation members and not all church musicians have anchored it, with all of its simplicity and promise, in that corner of their minds where they tuck images.

The people's song: connect it with a typical change in churchly imagery in our century. For instance: before the Second Vatican Council (1962–65), most images of the Roman Catholic church were of a "top down" character. There were an institution and a hierarchy with an authoritative if not authoritarian structure. The lay people, who were supposed to be served by it all, often turned out to be at the bottom of the organizational chart as those who served it, who existed for it.

Without doing away with hierarchy or institution—why should it? how could it?—Catholicism at Vatican II began to speak of a different image: *the people of God*. I cannot say that such a notion turned the chart upside down, but it certainly leads people to begin at the other end of the chart when they think about the church. The church is not some mystical ideal or some rough institution. It is *people*, specifically *people of God*. Their fundamental activity is worship, liturgy, the work of the people of God; it is *the people's service.* And they come to unity in praise by praying together and by singing together—led by the *cantor,* who helps produce *the people's song.*

Simple.

Yet it takes a good deal of thought. Paul Westermeyer has given the concept much thought, and passes on both his reflection and his vast experience to others. Most of these others are themselves cantors, or would-be cantors, no matter what their current or dreamed-of titles may be. They are a very powerful group. Lines two and three of Westermeyer's introduction suggest that: they lead "about forty-seven million people in song at worship each weekend." Their responsibilities among these forty-seven million people who sing the people's song are great. I mean no insult to them in their grand profession when I say, however, that this is too good a book to be wasted on merely a few tens of thousands of such cantors.

In his efforts to reach the church musicians Westermeyer uses the word *you.* He wants each reader to know that he is not talking about a performer far away, a great cathedral musician high in her or his loft, someone else. He is talking about and to *you.* Yet I think his book is for many other people as well: pastors, church staffs, congregational worship committees, theologians, seminarians, people of culture, and anyone who wants to understand praise, worship, and music.

The book would lose something if the author chose to write "to whom it may concern." But it takes only a few pages for non-musicians to learn that they can profit much from what is here. Picture being invited to eavesdrop on an important conversation, to overhear its nuances, to gather hints for oneself.

Among those who might profit from and would delight in this book are pastoral ministers of congregations. It will come as no surprise to many of them to learn that not all of them are popular with church musicians. A son and brother of church musicians and a sometimes pastor, I have spoken at local and national meetings of the American Guild of Organists and at church music professionals' workshops. Despite my experience I was surprised to hear as many expressions as I did of what has to be called anticlericalism, or at least deep resentment. The emotion is not universal: there are many thousands of satisfied and fulfilled musicians who are co-professional with pastors.

Sometimes the resentments have to do with what cannot be changed. Not all ministers can produce funds for great new organs, members for great big choirs, salaries that match what their musicians merit. But almost all ministers could be better partners in leading worship if they were better cooperators in planning, if they better understood the goals of worship leadership as church musicians, cantors, at their best understand them. Here is a guarantee: if the pastoral and musical leaders of your congregation read this book and do not find that it helps them, write me a letter (Swift Hall, The University of Chicago, 60637), and I'll consult Paul Westermeyer and engage in correspondence about the situation. We should live so long as to extend the guarantee through the third revised edition of 1998!

Christians have a long way to go in improving their worship, for the glory of God and the sensibilities of participants. Annie Dillard somewhere complains: we Christians have been artfully working at the act of worship, weekly, for two thousand years. Yet we are often more amateurish and inept than are the company and cast of the little local high school that has only a few weeks to rehearse its annual play. Westermeyer does not expect congregations to transcend their boundaries. This is not essentially a book for cathedrals and cantors who work with large, prestigious, paid choirs (though they will profit by reading it, too). He does not believe that there is only one cultural style, one aesthetic level, one musical mode that is God-pleasing and that will serve all congregations well. He does think that each congregation can learn what its own genius is, can establish new goals for expressing it, and can come closer to meeting those goals.

I believe that for the professional cantors, leaders of the people's song, organists, and others who read and reread this book, it can serve as far more than a "how-to" manual. Readers will almost certainly be drawn to the way the author lives with them through the hour and day of worship and then extends this sense of time through the week, the year, the passages of life, as it were. There is in this approach a discipline that will do far more for the cantors than merely helping them get better at their jobs, at advancing their careers, at developing their professions.

This is a book aimed at their vocations, their callings, their very lives. It helps them understand the story of which they, or the people they serve, are a vital part. That understanding comes as a bonus in this book. Maybe I should turn all that around: because the cantor learns a way of life to complement his or her natural gifts and training and experience, the increase in knowledge about the cantorial role, about church musicianship, is the bonus. And the people who sing and hear "the people's song" will benefit.

And now we have a welcome new edition of this book; welcome because it is an update in a time when regular updating is necessary in the face of changed cultural situations; new because the revisions and supplemental materials address circumstances faced by a new half-generation of church musicians, worship committees, pastors, planners, and congregants.

The old virtues of the older edition are here. Westermeyer cannot not speak humanely, with a sense of mastery of his subject, and with an empathy for church musicians in their many large and small, expansive or restrictive, encouraging or discouraging circumstances. As before, this book should be useful for anyone who tries to help give voice to the song of the believing congregants and to employ music not to entertain but to draw them to the center of what worship intends.

While the first edition was written in full consciousness that many modes of "doing" church music, traditional and contemporary alike, were being criticized or, worse, allowed to be misused or fallen into disuse, this edition must reflect a harsher, less civil, more polarized time.

Near the century's end, many citizens have begun to talk about "culture wars," drawing their concept from a book by James Davison Hunter. Taking off from there, numbers of listeners-in to debate in Christian circles, beginning with congregations, have spoken of "worship wars." One may not welcome the military metaphor, as I do not: it is hyperbolic—these are not real wars—and overdone as analogy. It tends to be favored by people who "take no prisoners," who have no room for compromise, who do not listen to each other and, frankly, among whom "the fruit of the spirit" spelled out in Galatians 5:22–23, is often forgotten in the interest of winning—what? What is a winner and how does one recognize and deal Christianly with the loser? Who gave one side the right, in the name of God, to declare the terms for battle, and to declare victory?

Often one side in a "culture war," a "worship war," any churchly battle, acts as if and even claims that God is on her side. Once that occurs, there is no more self-questioning of the sort we get in Westermeyer's writings and teaching. There is no room for efforts made to hear what the other represents or, again, frankly, to love the other. The partisans sometimes claim the mantle of the prophet: is not the Bible full of righteous and sure proclaimers? Look at Isaiah 58 for a sample, or turn to Jeremiah for more rigorous ones or Jesus overturning tables at the temple for still more vigorous taking of stands and making utterances or engaging in action to suggest that "there's a war on."

Westermeyer knows enough to know that there are not enough biblical spellings-out of what God wants by way of worship for us to be too sure. There may be clues. In the present "worship wars," for one side the market—a not really convincing measure of truth—dominates. Do in worship whatever draws a larger audience or congregation. For another side, the claims of tradition and integrity are so compelling that they will pay no attention to other biblical norms. No one profits.

I have pictured "culture wars" as I picture "worship wars." Imagine a figurative landscape that features two mesas with a valley between. Atop each is the heavy artillery of the partisans of the wars, the firers of heavy cannon aimed at the other. Much of the firing falls upon noncombatants who live in the valley of indecision, who can live with openness alongside evasion, with empathy alongside the ability to criticize, but who are marked most by the sense that they are unrepresented in the wars.

Take any vital issue, such as abortion. All polls suggest that 10–15% of the people are purely pro-life. Pure pro-life says "better two deaths than one murder." Take fetal life to save a mother's and you are already nonabsolutist, impure. On the other side or mesa-with-cannon are the polar opposite 10–15% who are purely pro-choice. For them, there are no life issues, no debates over the status and rights of the fetus. Only the mother's freedom to choose in isolation matters. Between them are 70–80% of the people, most of whom tell poll-takers that they are critical of or oppose abortion, but do not want to forbid it constitutionally or remove all choice from all women. They tend to take their position on one side or other of the valley in the light of who fired the most recent shot.

So with "worship wars." One camp is made up of utter traditionalists, leaders who wish they could be living in some previous century of high-quality liturgical practice and achievement. They know exactly what God wanted and thus wants; they always are infallible about what is good or bad, esthetically or theologically God-pleasing and appropriate and what is not. Give them 10–15% in the leadership and followership of the worshiping community. On the other mesa is a different 10–15% made up of utter pragmatists, leaders who claim to be living wholly in the now. They know exactly what will draw a crowd; they are relativists about what is "good or bad," at least esthetically and perhaps theologically, when it comes to the God-pleasing. God is pleased if more people show up and immediately like what is going on, whether by any standard what they are doing is tawdry, sloppy, ephemeral, or out of context.

Between them are believers who are ready to listen for the voice of tradition in efforts to link with the people of God across time, yet who know that sensibilities change and culture does determine much of who we are and what we understand and enjoy and how we worship. Give that valley full 70–80% of the leadership and congregational membership.

There are plenty of leaders on both sides in culture wars or worship wars. There are too few who will sound trumpets, provide cover, assist those "in-between" to find and employ standards. Paul Westermeyer is one of the leaders who in this book is trying to equip others. He is a gentle, reasoning, listening soul, who has been attentive to biblical and theological norms as he is alert to cultural limitations and possibilities in our time. He prefers to deal with those who disagree with him on that broad plain, not in absolutist or uncompromising terms but in situations of conversation where they can reason with each other and provide intelligent and God-pleasing leadership in worship. This book can be seen as a carrying on of that conversation, without a trace of wishy-washiness or dogmatism. Yet convictions are here, along with rationales for them.

The new material focuses on this aspect of the situation. I wish Westermeyer and those for whom he writes did not have to spend so much time in providing rationales and apologias. I wish they could put all their time into writing, presenting and leading music and worship. But it is clear that many are defenseless against those who want numbers of adherents to be the only, or almost the only, and certainly the privileged criterion for what is to "go" in worship. He avoids the whining tone, always an ineffective one, and instead takes up one or another of the assaults against the integrity of worship music as he hears it, and responds.

He will not get a hearing from the culture warriors or the worship warriors. To absolutists in one camp he will sound too "contemporary," too "compromised"; to those in another he will sound too "traditional," too "uncompromising."

Which situates him exactly where he ought to be and wants to be: among the still too rare company of leaders for the majority of God's people who would sing the Lord's song and the New song in the ever more strange land in which we find ourselves. I hope he gets the fresh hearing that he deserves. We'll all hear better, and sound better, by any standard, if he does, and is heeded.

Martin E. Marty

Introduction

ACROSS THE LENGTH AND BREADTH of the United States a remarkable group of musicians leads about 47 million persons in
song at worship each weekend. These people are usually called
choir directors, organists, directors of music, ministers of music,
soloists, and a variety of other names. Sometimes they have no
title and simply emerge in assembly as leaders by their presence
and gifts. They represent an extremely wide array of abilities,
training, practice and skills. Some have degrees, including doc-
torates, and have spent their lives learning about and practicing
their craft. Others have little or no training, but use whatever
abilities and tools lay at hand. A few are paid quite well for their
efforts. Most are paid poorly, many not at all. Some have full-time
positions; others work half-time or in some part-time capacity.

This book concerns all these musical leaders who serve God
and the people of God through music. All these leaders, whatever
their background and station, share a common task. Recent currents of liturgical renewal and concerns in churches about worship in relation to the culture have heightened and accented that
task. But too often musicians and the people they serve are un-
aware, not only of the newly heightened task, but of the task itself
and its importance. My intent is to bring the role of the church
musician to conscious awareness and to focus and define that im-

1

portant but often misunderstood role. I hope these ideas will be helpful to musicians, pastors, and congregations who have already thought about them. For these people the book may serve to recall what they already know and stimulate new insights. Mostly, however, these ideas are intended for those who have not thought much about them, but who now want or need to do so.

When I first wrote this book two groups of people inspired it. One consisted of pastors or members of music committees, from whom I still receive almost weekly calls, looking for musicians for their churches. Sometimes these people know exactly what is needed, why it is needed, and what kind of musician might serve their needs. More often, however, they have at best only a vague sense of what the search is about. Their common underlying and unarticulated theme sounds like a cry: "Help! Could you tell me briefly what the real role of the church musician is?"

The other group was church musicians or would-be church musicians who have little background and training. When I conduct workshops for these people, I can see that they hunger for some perspective on the role of the church musician. They need a quick overview of this perspective, in order to begin to see the dimensions of the job with some clarity. With that need in mind, I wrote the book as tersely as possible, providing little detail and amplification. And I wrote it directly to these musicians, often lapsing into the second person as if speaking to them at a workshop. I hoped pastors and music committees and the rest of the church would sense that I was really addressing their needs as well, even when I was speaking to the musicians themselves. Pastors were often and may well still be the first to see this and read it. I hoped, and still hope, that they will want to share it with the musicians and music committees in their churches.

Many of the people who read the first edition were church musicians or students planning to be full-time church musicians. They often had quite a bit of background and training, but needed to think out some basic presuppositions of their existence and found these thoughts helpful. They found this need even more pressing during recent attacks on their roles and contributions in the church. I had these people in mind as well in this revision, especially in the last chapter.

A number of friends and acquaintances from a variety of traditions and backgrounds have reviewed various portions and drafts of this book: Robert J. Batastini, Walter R. Bouman, Robert Brusic, Gary B. Butler, Susan Cherwien, Melva W. Costen, Carol Doran, Hedda Durnbaugh, Harry Eskew, John Ferguson, Robert A. Hausman, C. Michael Hawn, John C. Helt, Donald P. Hustad, T. Howard Krueger, Paul Landahl, Robin Leaver, David W. Music, Ronald A. Nelson, Paul A. Richardson, Naomi Rowley, Gordon Rowley, Don E. Saliers, Carl Schalk, Robert Scholz, Thomas H. Troeger, W. Thomas Smith, Robert E. Webber, John Witvliet and Carlton R. Young. Francis Williamson, a fellow church musician and retired college professor with whom I have had discussions for years about these matters, made some of the most challenging comments both for the first and second editions. All of these people offered valuable advice. In some cases I have followed their suggestions; in some cases I have not. None of these readers is in any way responsible for the final product, which is my own, but I am grateful for their cogent and lively responses and for their gracious help. They have affirmed what I said, but also challenged me to look at things in other ways, or to say things more precisely, or to consider nuances I did not see.

I owe a special word of thanks to Martin E. Marty, who graciously wrote the foreword. I know him not only as my doctoral adviser, but also as a remarkably perceptive and caring churchman, historian, and human being. As he did for my dissertation, here again he helped me sort out my thoughts to say what I wanted to say. I am deeply grateful to him for his help, concern, and understanding.

I am also grateful to two deans and two schools. John Bohnert, my former dean, and Elmhurst College provided sabbatical time to complete and revise the first edition of this project. Daniel Simundson was the dean at Luther Seminary when sabbatical time was granted for work on this second edition.

Finally, to Linda Huebner, secretary and receptionist extraordinaire, my thanks for duplicating, collating, and sending—beyond the call of duty.

Church musicians are a hearty, creative band of delightful folk who are engaged in a task more important than they know. They are leaders in worship. Our culture tends to lump them together with all other musicians as entertainers, missing the real significance of their work. I hope I can communicate a reality they know but often are not able to articulate. And I hope that their lives and the lives of those they serve will become more rewarding and meaningful because of it.

Chapter 1

Music Grinder

SUNDAY MORNING ROLLS AROUND AGAIN. You are half awake before the alarm goes off. In that half-dream, half-reality world, you vaguely recall last week's grind at the office and Saturday night's party when you tried to forget the grind. And then you realize it's Sunday morning and time for your church job.

You had some skills as a pianist and even studied a little organ in college. Three years ago, when your friend in the church across town told you they needed an organist, you checked into the job. It seemed worth pursuing. You could serve God and the church, make a few extra dollars, challenge yourself to practice, and perhaps even gain some new skills. So you stopped attending your church around the corner and took the job across town.

For the first two years or so you renewed old skills and developed new ones as an organist. You even took some lessons at the junior college. You were pleased with your progress, and the people of the church appreciated your efforts. But in the last six months or so you've begun to feel more comfortable with your technical skills (even the feet are working pretty well), and the challenge is gone. You're acclimated; the people take you for granted now; you're playing the same literature a second (or third or fourth) time; you practice less; and now you push the same pistons every Sunday.

5

As you wake up on this Sunday morning, it suddenly strikes you that you are settling in as the music grinder of this church. If you're in for the long haul, you realize you'll have to keep dealing with the foibles of the minister (who pretty much leaves you alone), the choir director (with whom you sometimes mildly disagree), choir members (especially the obnoxious alto and her snide remarks), the council (including the new president who worries you), and the people of the congregation (who are generally supportive). You suddenly realize that none of those people you have to deal with seems to know what your role is. And you don't either! You obviously are supposed to play the organ—but why? They've always had an organ and organist. Is that enough reason? You're one of the church's music grinders, hired to grind out music the way the cook at the fast-food place in the shopping center is hired to grind out hamburgers. As you wake up you ask yourself if you really want to add a weekend grind to your weekly one at the office.

By changing some details, virtually every church musician in the country can probably identify with that illustration. Maybe you don't have an office job, but are a homemaker. Maybe you never studied organ and were pressed (unwillingly?) into service in your own church. Perhaps you are a composer who only took the church job because you could not support yourself as a composer alone. Maybe you are the choir director, song leader, or soloist, and not the organist at all. Maybe you play the piano, or maybe it's guitar in a jazz combo at one service. Whatever you do, at one time or another you probably asked yourself why you were doing it. You saw this ghost of music grinder going through the motions, and you wondered what your role really was supposed to be.

Many factors create and sustain the existence of music grinders, and they work against your fulfilling your real role as a church musician. The culture itself does it. We live in a culture in which musicians can find excellent technical training, but the unspoken presupposition is always that musicians are entertainers. The nature of the entertainment may vary widely, from symphony orchestra to opera to rock concert, to dance hall to popular recordings to television commercials and elevator music. Some of this music may be called edifying rather than entertaining, and some of it may be considered trivial. But the church musician as church musician (not as concert artist or performer) doesn't really fit any of these categories and can easily begin to feel like a second-class citizen.

Second-class citizenship and poor self-image are underlined by cultural stereotypes: the cheap electronic organ with the same boring sounds and the same music played over and over; the much maligned church choir, held up as an object of ridicule by symphony chorus conductors who want to shame their professional choruses into shape; mediocre compositions fostered and protected by churches. Though some churches have excellent pipe organs with superb music programs, some of the finest choirs in the world are church choirs, and some churches will not tolerate mediocrity, the stereotypes are often all too true to be denied. They do not do much for a church musician's self-image, and they serve to foster music grinders who themselves fall into the stereotypical traps.

Curiously enough, the American church itself fosters music grinders. All mainstream denominations and most local churches regard a full-time pastor or priest as the norm, but to think of a full-time musician as normative would shock them. The musician in the vast majority of cases is part-time, both in theory and practice.

This situation means the church musician is usually not paid well. The music budget itself is often too low to allow much creativity. Money speaks and points to priorities. The musician looks at the pay and music budget, and sees second-class music grinder written all over them. Not only do these factors affect self-image; the musician has to have food and shelter like everyone else. If serving as a church musician cannot generate enough money, a full-time job elsewhere is the only alternative. The church job has to be the second job. It's moonlighting, money on the side, worked into the cracks of time, and grind.

Paradoxically, music inevitably accompanies the Christian church even when institutional supports for it are not provided. One would expect the leaders, the clergy, therefore to have some knowledge of the church's song, even when money for music is short. Part-time musicians ought to be able to ask full-time pastors at least for resources about church music. But that is seldom the case and again creates music grinders. Despite some delightful exceptions, American clergy generally know little about church music, hymnody, and even worship. Part-time musicians, even ones with little training, often know more about these topics than do clergy. This statement is not so much an indictment of the clergy as it is an indictment of American seminaries. For most seminaries, church music, hymnody, and even worship as disciplines of study have been sandwiched into a corner or avoided altogether. Music grinders are one result. The musician finds it difficult to view his or her terrain as important when it is neglected in the training of the full-time leaders, which is true even though the musician's terrain—church music, hymnody, and worship—touches the people most directly.

The realities of culture and institutional church conspire to keep the church musician a music grinder in more ways than the ones just suggested. Part-time church musicians are notoriously short on time. The full-time job which pays the bills takes most of the time each week. The part-time church job often has to be forced into the cracks of the week when one is likely to be tired. Planning, practice, and study have to be done on the run. In some cases they are not done at all, with expected results—like cringing congregations.

What to do for training is another problem. Some denominations have workshops—often in the summer—for musicians. Colleges sometimes sponsor workshops; training in organ and choral technique is usually readily available at a college, university, or extension program; and some colleges have church music programs. Organizations such as the Hymn Society in the United States and Canada (HS) and the American Guild of Organists (AGO) provide helpful publications and programs.

Books and knowledgeable people are also available. The list of options sounds long and varied, but it narrows quickly and has its problems.

Denominational workshops are the only built-in possibilities. Not all denominations have them, however, and while they can be extremely valuable, they are necessarily brief and cannot provide sustained instruction and practice over a long period, which all disciplines—especially music—require.

You must search out all the other possibilities. Your church and pastor are not likely to know about them and may not even pass on to you announcements that publicize them. The musician has to take the initiative, and sometimes that is hard. I have discovered many church musicians who could be helped by college workshops, lessons, the HS and the AGO, but who are afraid to participate for fear they are not good enough or not worthy enough. The fear is misplaced, of course, since those opportunities are there for all of us. We are all worthy of them, no matter what our background or training. They lead to resources, books, and people and provide the collegiality that stimulates growth and allows us to learn about common problems. Fear of participating means no growth and perpetuates music grinders.

When you conquer the fear, you then confront the realities of time and money. Workshops may be scheduled during a family vacation or when you have to work. Lessons or classes may be at difficult times in the week and may require driving some distance. Most of these options also cost money. If you don't yet have the church job or the church won't support your desire to learn, the money comes out of your pocket, and may be hard to come by. These matters can be solved, of course, if one has the will to solve them. Until they are solved, however, they stand as barriers to the fulfillment of your real role as a church musician.

The kind of training I have been discussing relates primarily, though not only, to the part-time church musician, which means most of us. If you plan to fight the odds and want to join that small minority of full-time church musicians, another kind of training is obviously required. Ideally, you will want a bachelor's degree from a college with a church music program or a music major that includes courses in church music. Then you will want a master's degree at a school with a church music degree. Some (few) denominations have these, and some universities also have good ecumenical programs. Obviously, this route requires large doses of talent, time, and money—plus an inner compulsion that will not wane. It is for the hardy, and you need to know when you enter it that a full-time position may be hard to find even if you are well-trained.

We have described the culture, the institutional church, and problems in training as three large forces that can easily conspire to keep you a music grinder. One final area has to do with issues of faith. The commercial musician, the dance musician, the orchestral player, and the baseball organist all can view their jobs as callings. They can—and should—have a sense of vocation. But they don't have to believe in what they do the way the church musician does. In this sense the church musician is unique among musicians.

The church musician is always dealing with a community of faith. What you do as a musician in the church relates to what the people believe. The song you lead is the song of their faith. To avoid this issue is to predetermine grind. It is possible to crank out music for money in any context, including the church, but it is never very rewarding.

This question of faith may suggest that only the "true believer" can be the church musician, that a member of the congregation is the only possible candidate for the post. To have a member of the community of faith serve that community as the musician is indeed a happy solution, provided the person possesses the proper talents and skills. The proper talents and skills are not always present in the community, however, and our pluralistic society causes so much movement across communities of faith that congregations themselves have many varieties of "true believers." Church musicians therefore often serve churches other than their own.

One has to be careful here, for matters of faith are not to be taken lightly. They are precious treasures. But it is possible for a person from one community of faith to serve another as the musician. Three things are necessary. First, you need a sense of your own faith or at least some idea of where you are in your pilgrimage. Second, you need to know what the people you serve believe. And, third, you must be able to enter with empathy into their experience.

You need not and should not suspend your beliefs. If matters of conscience cause impossible conflicts, you cannot take or keep the position, of course. But confessional lines can be crossed so long as the three preceding requirements are met.

Obviously, enough forces exist to keep you a music grinder. But, as I have been intimating, there is also another possibility. To that we now turn.

Chapter 2

Cantor

DON'T LET THE TITLE OF THIS CHAPTER stop you from reading on. You may not have encountered the term *cantor* before except in the context of a Jewish synagogue, or perhaps in a reference to J. S. Bach, or possibly as a quite specific designation among Roman Catholics. The term's definition and implications, however, help get at some essential points. So read on for the essentials.

I propose to call the church musician *cantor* because that term highlights the people's song. And that is what we are mainly about here.

Cantor comes from the Latin word *cantare* or *canere*, which means to sing. It refers to the chief singer, the person who leads the people in singing. Like so many other things in Christian worship—forms of prayer, lessons, the Liturgy of the Word itself—Christians may derive the term from the Jewish synagogue.[1]

---

1. The derivation, origin, and meaning of the term *cantor* are confusing and tangled. Sources that raise the issues include the following: Edward Foley, "The Cantor in Historical Perspective," *Worship* 56:3 (May 1982): 194–213, revised in *Ritual Music* (Beltsville: The Pastoral Press, 1995), 65-87; Edward Foley, "The Role of the Cantor," *The American Organist* 17:9 (September 1983): 64–65; Mark Bangert, "Ministers of the Merger," *Church Music Memo* 43 (1986): 2–7; Francis H. Williamson, "The Lord's Song and the Ministry of the Church" (Th.D. diss., Union Theological Seminary, 1967), 90–92.

There the cantor is an important worship leader, the one who leads the singing. Contemporary society tends to view a cantor as a great voice like Robert Merrill, Richard Tucker, or Jan Peerce who developed from the Jewish cantorial tradition into opera stars. Many Jewish cantors have had great voices, of course, but the quality of their voice is secondary to the primary meaning of leading the song.

Both the Jewish and the Christian cantor developed from voluntary musical leadership in worship.[2] In the church either lay persons or clergy originally assumed this role. As monastic and cathedral services became more elaborate and clergy-dominated in the medieval West, the cantor turned into an essential fixture of the liturgy's proper execution. Careful rules were laid out. In the process the cantor became more and more divorced from the people's song and the term *cantor* more and more restricted to clerical and choral functions. *Precentor* and *succentor*, for instance, are clergy in cathedral and collegiate Anglican churches. Both terms derive from *cantor.* The precentor, literally *the one who sings before,* directs the choral service. The precentor's deputy is the succentor or *subcantor.*

The Puritans also used the term *precentor,* but with a meaning somewhat nearer its synagogal origins and literal sense. The precentor set the pitch of the Psalms and led their singing or, later, lined out the Psalms for the people. (Lining out is a practice in which one person reads or sings a line, followed by the people's singing of the same line. It developed where people could not read or did not have hymnals.) Contemporary Roman Catholics use the term *cantor* in a similar way, to refer to a singer who leads the people or alternates with them in specific sung portions of the Mass, especially the psalmody.[3] In the German Lutheran tradition the cantor was in charge of music for the congregation, music and musical instruction in the school, and music for the city. He was responsible for the people's singing of

---

2. Cf. Foley, *Ritual Music,* 66.
3. See James Hansen, *The Ministry of the Cantor* (Collegeville: The Liturgical Press, 1985).

the liturgy and hymns; directed the *Kantorei* and deployed its vocal and instrumental forces as needed in church, school, and city; and composed *Gebrauchsmusik*—occasional music—for weddings, funerals, and civic functions along with pieces for services throughout the church year, such as cantatas. Johann Walter, Johann Eccard, Johann Crüger, and J. S. Bach were all cantors.[4]

Even when their basis was forgotten, all of these usages pointed in practice to a common heritage—the people's song. Most contemporary terms for the church musician, on the other hand, point either to a post-Enlightenment mentality in which music is for entertaining, or to a neutral conception that relates to music alone. Our terms do not point to the role of the church musician in the body of Christ.

Choir director, for instance, suggests the one who directs a choir for an audience of listeners, which is a most legitimate role, but not the essence of the church musician's responsibility. *Organist* suggests a keyboard player who plays organ literature while the people listen. Again, that is a legitimate and important role, but not the essence of a church musician. *Soloist* especially connotes concert performance. *Director of Music* suggests the one who coordinates a program of music, usually of the concert variety. Sometimes we informally use the term *musician*, as in "the Methodist musician in Collinsville." None of these terms relates primarily to the people's song.

Minister of Music is one term we use in our attempts to point specifically to the church musician's role, but it reflects our confusion. We have often been reminded in our generation that all Christians are *ministers*. Such a definition, though true, leaves us with no notion of why some people are designated as laity and others as clergy. When you consider the distinction, you invariably come to some variation on the theme that ministers in the sense of clergy are responsible for preaching the Word and administering the Sacraments. *Minister of Music* obviously does not fit this definition, so it has to fit a more general sense and sug-

---

4. See Herbert Neuchterlein, "Cantor," *Key Words in Church Music*, Carl Schalk, ed. (St. Louis: Concordia Publishing House, 1978), 45–47.

gests that a particular Christian, possibly but not necessarily ordained, is literally responsible for serving up the music.[5] The title *Minister of Music* may imply ministry or ministry through music to others, but it neglects reference to the people's song, which is what calls the church musician into being in the first place and defines his or her primary obligation.

Pastoral musician may be closer to the mark because it highlights the pastoral significance of the church musician. Again, however, even though *pastoral* presumes an office on behalf of the people, it can be too easily understood to sidestep the people's song.

The term *cantor* rescues us from this dilemma. It also points us to the practices and concepts of early Christianity. As James F. White indicates in his *Introduction to Christian Worship*, looking to the early church characterizes much of contemporary Christianity, and future ages will have to judge whether we have "too easily romanticized the early period."[6] Whether we have or not, early Christianity provides an ecumenical route around our denominational impasses and is fodder for much of our cross-denominational liturgical renewal, which may explain why the term cantor is being used with increasing frequency.

Does the term itself make any difference? Can't one be called *organist* or *director* and still fulfill a cantorial role? Of course one can. I worked out the logic of using the term *cantor* for the church musician twenty years before I ever held a position called *cantor*. Before that I was always called *choir director* or *choirmaster-organist*. I fulfilled what I thought was a cantorial role, nevertheless, even though I was not called *cantor*. And many—perhaps most—church musicians probably do precisely the same thing. But both a symbolic and a practical value can be found in being called what you are. Symbolically, a title participates in the reality to which it points, and it also signifies that reality to church and world. Practically (the symbol is, of course, already profoundly practical), a job description will be far closer to the mark

5. Mark Bangert, "Ministers of the Merger," 3.

6. James F. White, *Introduction to Christian Worship*, Revised Edition (Nashville: Abingdon, 1990), 15.

and simpler to fashion if the title itself is close to the mark.

You can do what you have to do no matter what you are called, and I do not mean to be a legalist about titles. Since the term *cantor* does imply so much that I mean to imply for the church musician, however, I will tend to use the term for the remainder of the book. If it does not feel comfortable for you, feel free to substitute your own title or designation.

Who then is the cantor or chief singer among us? In our culture it is often the organist who may not actually sing at all, but who leads hymns and the liturgy. Organists in our period like Paul Manz, John Ferguson, David Cherwien, Mark Sedio, and Michael Burkhardt are good examples. In some cases it may be the choir director or song leader who conducts the congregation. Mary Oyer, Kenneth Nafziger, Alice Parker, and John Bell are good examples. It may be the conductor of the choir who thereby exerts control over the congregational song. It may be the cantor who alternates or sings with the people as Roman Catholic usage suggests. It may be the guitar player or instrumental group who leads the singing. It may be the director of music who oversees all these leaders of the people, or it may be several of these leaders together who constitute a cantorial staff. *Cantor*, as I am using it, encompasses all these meanings. It denotes the person or persons who lead the people in song, however it is done.

To lead the people in song is at once simple and complex. It is a marvelously varied affair. It may mean leading a small congregation in an unaccompanied unison line, or it may mean leading a large assembly with choirs, bands, and orchestras in polyrhythmic and polytonal complexity. Men or women can do it, and those with the most creative capacities will never cease to be challenged by it. It encompasses the simplest amateur expression and the most perfect possible professional performance. It is for the part-time amateur and the full-time J. S. Bach. And it is one of the most rewarding things you will ever do.

Chapter 3

Getting Started

WHEN THINGS ARE REDUCED to their simplest terms, what does the cantor need? Two broad needs are equally important: knowing the story and having the capacity to make music with the people.

Knowing the Story

First, the cantor needs to know the story. We often view churches as groups that hold doctrines or beliefs. Churches split over doctrines, and what one faction holds to be true deviates from another. We can tell one denomination from another by its beliefs. Behind the beliefs, however, is a story. It is this fundamental story that first must claim the cantor's attention.

G. Ernest Wright wrote a book he called *God Who Acts: Biblical Theology as Recital*.[1] In it he pointed to the Biblical story of what God has done. Gabriel Fackre, in *The Christian Story: A Narrative Interpretation of Basic Christian Doctrine*, "unfolds the Christian faith in the form of story."[2] Both Wright and Fackre pre-

---

1. G. Ernest Wright, *God Who Acts: Biblical Theology as Recital* (London: SCM Press LTD, 1952).

2. Gabriel Fackre, *The Christian Story: A Narrative Interpretation of Basic Christian Doctrine,* (Grand Rapids: William B. Eerdmans Publishing Company, 1984) rev. ed., 1.

sent the central story to which the cantor must attend. It is the story of creation; of human rebellion against the love of God; of deliverance from bondage in Egypt; of covenant; of prophets who speak God's searing Word of love and judgment; of just and wise yet rebellious kings; of the Word made flesh—God among us as teacher, servant, crucified and risen Lord; of the church as Christ's body, adopted, redeemed, filled with the Spirit, flowing into space and history to be what Christ was, yet failing and forgiven; of a broken, hungry, warring yet celebrative world in need of the love the creator of the universe so graciously offers; and of a human history above which and beyond which stands the love of God in Christ in spite of all appearances to the contrary.

Theologians, preachers, and common Christian folk have joyously agonized over that amazing story. We have picked it apart detail by detail. We still ask what each detail means. One generation emphasizes one facet, another generation something else. One group points to one theme as most important, another group finds that theme less meaningful and fastens on yet another. All of us ride our own hobbyhorses. It is easy to get lost in specific details and lose sight of the plot.

The cantor cannot lose sight of the plot. She or he is not called to know every theological detail nor to unravel every theological question. The cantor as cantor is called to keep the whole story in perspective and to know its broad outlines and major themes. This call should not be understood to mean that the cantor is tied to the latest theological fad nor to any single hermeneutical (interpretative) perspective. The point here is not that the story is defined as *Heilsgeschichte* (which is out of fashion) nor in the categories of more recent story approaches. The point here is that individual songs from scripture and tradition always be placed in the context of the whole story, which moves from creation to consummation, and that they tell all or part of that story. To understand and be responsible for the song, one must know and understand the story. The psalms, for example, only make sense in the context of the history of the Israelites. J.S. Bach's Cantata 140 *(Wachet auf)* only makes sense if one understands it was composed for the end of the church year and anticipates the Advent themes of Christ's original and final coming. The spiritual, "O Mary, don't you weep, don't you mourn, Pharaoh's army got drownded," only makes sense if one understands that Mary and the oppressed whom she represents are being comforted by the knowledge that in Christ death has been conquered, and the victory of Israel over Pharaoh at the Red Sea is related to the victory of Christ over death. The key to every canticle, hymn, anthem, passion, motet, cantata, and spiritual is finding its place in the story.

The cantor also needs to know a context and a derivative story. The context is the cultural setting, particularly its musical part, which forms and shapes the way we hear and sing. Learning about the culture requires listening with discrimination to what is present all around us—on the radio and television, in concert halls, in shopping malls, on recordings. You don't simply embrace all of that, but you need to know about it. Learning about the culture also requires knowing the heritage of a specific people. If you serve an African American parish, for example, the speech patterns, inflections, and musical ear of the people will differ from those of a Slovak or Hispanic congregation. Those speech patterns, inflections, and ways of hearing are not arbitrary whims. They spring from the ethnicity and heritage of a people. The cantor works within the context of how people speak, hear, and therefore sing. Knowing the context is no small matter.

The derivative story has two components. One is made up of individual stories with all the personal struggles and joys which attend our lives. The second is the story of the congregation you serve, which both includes and transcends the individuals who form it.

You learn individual stories gradually and gently as you live with the people over a long period of time. This learning cannot be forced and comes as relationships of trust are established. One finds that the personal laments and songs of thanksgiving in the Psalms have special relevance here to help people give voice to their own anguish and joys. The cantor is the psalmist for whom the Psalms are of critical importance. They are remarkable in that they not only serve the needs of corporate worship, but also express the sorrows and delights of individuals as well.

> My God, my God,
>> why have you forsaken me
>> Why are so far from helping me,
>>> from the words of my groaning?
>>>> (Psalm 22:1)

> You have turned my mourning into dancing;
>> you have put off my sackcloth
>> and clothed me with joy.
> so that my soul may praise you and not be silent.
>> O Lord my God, I will give thanks to you forever.
>>> (Psalm 30:11-12)

Learning the history of a people also comes little by little, but it is easier to get at. You learn it by asking questions, by observing and listening, by being present in social and other gatherings. You can tell a great deal about a people's story by looking at their church building. When was it built? Why is the altar where it is? Do they call it an altar or a table? Why does it look the way it does? Where is the pulpit? How big is it? How is it designed? Why? Who made the banners? Why are they designed that way? When were they made? Why? Looking through the choral library or at past bulletins will also tell you many things: what kind of music the congregation and choir have sung, what pieces they used often and which ones very little, what kind of texts they use, what sort of style and sound is in their ears, how worship is understood. You will find contradictions and incongruities that characterize all histories, but you will also find a coherence that tells you how this people has been shaped, how they have translated the great story into their language, and how their story is part of the larger plot.

You need to know the story of God's mighty acts, a derivative story, and the context. And you must be responsive to all these elements. Without the big story the whole enterprise is hopeless, and without the little story and the context, you work in a vacuum.

Developing Technical Skills

The second broad need of the cantor is the capacity to do the music-making with the people. It means sufficient native ability, technical training, and practice—in ascending order of importance.

The point here is not that every cantor needs to be a musical genius. Geniuses are welcomed to the cantorial role, but so are those of us with meager or moderate abilities. The critical thing is that the cantor possess the skills requisite to his or her situation. Simplicity is not necessarily a vice, nor complexity a virtue. The people's song in a particular time and place should be the center and control. Skills and techniques must serve that specific song. The cantor must develop the skills and techniques for that specific service.

It should be emphasized that the skills and techniques must be developed. Anything less than excellence is extremely disruptive to worship. This requirement creates one of the cantor's special tensions to which I shall return. For now let me simply make the point.

Another point must be emphasized: the amateur with little time and meager abilities can develop the necessary skills just as the professional with much time and many abilities. For both persons, continuing practice is mandatory and critical. If skills are matched to responsibilities and situations, each person can do an admirable job. The difference here is simply one of degree, not kind. Neither is better than the other. The task for both persons is the same: serve the people, and practice sufficiently to be able to do it well.

Knowing the story and developing the skills to lead the song are life-long projects. The story is so rich in meaning that it can never be fully understood, and its implications are new every morning. The skills can never be fully developed, for with each skill you learn, a whole new set is suggested and needs to be worked out.

At first glance this cycle may seem frustrating. Actually it suggests the delight of the cantor's role. There is always something new to learn, something new to do, a new hymn, a new anthem, a new harmonization, a new skill, a new insight, a new tone color or tempo, something stimulating that suggests another way to understand and express the song. Life-long learning is built into the cantor's responsibility—learning as varied as the designs of a kaleidoscope.

When to Begin

Since the cantor's learning is life-long, it carries another implication: you can begin any time—like now. You need enough understanding of the story and enough skills to serve a given people. Some high school students can do that in some situations, and, indeed, many church organists and choir directors begin in high school. The way to learn this craft is by doing it, and at some point you simply need to take the plunge.

It is best to find a teacher. The country is full of able church musicians who also teach. They are usually called organists, choir directors, directors of music, or choirmasters. These people teach in colleges, universities, and churches throughout the land. You can also hear them, even if you don't study with them, by going to their workshops or to services at which they are leading the song.

Finding a Job

Having done the necessary study to get started, how do you find a job? In *A Musician's Guide to Church Music*, Joy Lawrence and John Ferguson have authored an excellent chapter on the specifics of this search. They cover the following: developing your philosophy of sacred music, assessing your potential, putting together a resume, interviewing and auditioning, and evaluating the position you are offered.[3] I recommend their advice. It is clear and helpful. Here let me emphasize only one thing.

---

3. Joy E. Lawrence and John A. Ferguson, *A Musician's Guide to Church Music* (New York: The Pilgrim Press, 1981), 174–184.

The church musician is part of a community. You don't become part of a community by classified advertisements. You do it by engagement with two sets of people—other church musicians and the community or communities you will serve. You put yourself in touch with your fellow church musicians by joining the American Guild of Organists, the Hymn Society, the American Choral Directors Association, the Choristers Guild, a denominational organization of musicians, or a similar group. There you learn about your craft from others who are doing it, and you also hear of openings. To be engaged with the community you may serve, you must go where the action is, to a worship service if possible. A visit to a service will tell you more than many conversations, as will a visit to the church building. You need the conversations, of course, but there is no substitute for the actual experience.

Churches call me weekly or more in their search for organists and/or directors. Many positions are available. They run the gamut from small to large, from those with few responsibilities to those with many, offering little pay to respectable pay, and requiring from few to considerable abilities. Many churches do not know what they need, do not pay enough, and would be shocked to read a book like this one. Since the educational institutions of the church generally do such a poor job of training people for the role of the church musician or preparing pastors or churches to understand that role, one cannot expect churches to be aware of what they need. It is only when they wrestle with the issues that they realize what is required. Individual church musicians or even would-be church musicians come to their aid as best they can to help them wrestle. You may have to be one of those, even before you are engaged by a church. In applying for a position you can anticipate that you will probably be required to help the church bring to consciousness what it unconsciously knows it needs, but has never thoughtfully confronted.

Anticipating Problems

Once you have taken a position, you are likely to be welcomed graciously by the people. Unless some traumatic experience has occurred relative to your position or predecessor, and usually even then, the people will be genuinely grateful for your presence and will want to help you. But you may face some problems. Anticipate them, and you may keep them from getting out of hand.

First, schedules or traditions or practices, which make no sense to you or to anyone else, may be in place. You may not be able to figure out why they exist. Congregations are often like the woman who cut off the roast before putting it in the oven because her mother did it. Mother did it because *her* mother did it, and *she* did it because *her* mother did it. Nobody knew why until someone asked great-grandmother, who said she only did it because her oven was too small! The church may originally have had good reasons for practices which now make no sense. Churches are like people or families. (Churches *are* people and families!) We all are creatures of habit and perpetuate traditions that have lost their meaning.

On the other hand, traditions can bear a great deal of meaning not readily apparent at first glance, but on further inspection, rich and full of significance. For example, some form of the greeting, "The peace of the Lord be with you always" with its response "And also with you," remained in liturgies for centuries after the actual kiss of peace that had accompanied it in early church practice had been discontinued. Many twentieth century churches have rediscovered the rich meaning in this exchange and have re-instituted it in some form, as in a handshake or an embrace. The practical import of this inertia that accompanies the church's worship is to suggest you investigate what is in motion with the leaders of the parish. You *can* make changes, and you *ought* to make changes. But you have to do it sensitively with others and with an understanding of the people's story and needs. Some practices are pointless and should be scuttled. Scuttle them at the appropriate time. Remember, however, that you are not the sole arbiter of meaning nor the sole decision maker. You are part of a community of meaning whose story is richer and more varied than any one person can ever know and extends beyond any one generation.

Second, you will be dealing with volunteers. Even if you have a choir of professionals, volunteers sing in the congregation, are led by the professionals, and stand behind the professionals. That reality means two things. Volunteers are like amateurs in the best sense—they love what they do. You always have the possibility therefore for enormous interest, which can surprise you with its force. On the other hand, volunteers find their voluntary time more and more choked off in our economy, and they may be weary. They also can view themselves as too lacking in talent to do anything, especially if it's musical. This notion is wrong, of course, for to be human is to sing, but our culture perpetuates the notion that only geniuses can participate in musical activities. These problems can be solved, though no simple solution can be prescribed. Your role as cantor is to serve the people in your situation and to figure out what ought to happen there. Everybody can sing, and Christians of all sorts—with and without talent—have a song to sing. Your task is to figure out how to give it expression.

Third, economic issues cannot be avoided. Your salary will probably be too small, and your budget for music, musicians, instruments, and anything else you need will only rarely be adequate. Budgets can be increased, and a church's awareness of musical needs can be expanded where the resources are available. But you don't achieve those goals by worrying about money. Like disciplined athletes who do their job without whining, you do your job by doing it, not by crying about what you don't have. You can do all sorts of things within the limitations of any budget. Do them. Analyze the needs and potential of the people you serve within the confines of their resources. The culture tells you nothing can happen without mountains of money and glitter. The church knows another reality. All you really need are people, your creativity, and the Spirit of God. God gives the poorest people a song to sing. Help them sing it.

Fourth, musicians are artists, artists have ideals, and artists tend to regard less than their ideal as a compromise of conscience. The cantor needs to be careful here. The cantor is an artist, and the ideal of the artist is important to the cantor; but, unlike the secular artist, the cantor is not responsible in the final analysis to some arbitrary principle of perfection. The cantor's control is not a principle at all; it is the incarnation. The incarnation means, among other things, that God did not hold perfect divinity aloof from us, but "compromised" to take on our imperfect humanity. The compromise is so beneficial for us that the Cappadocian fathers could say, "Christ became human so that we could be divine."

"Compromising" has two implications for the cantor. First, the people's song is not produced by a single artist. It is produced by a community of normal human folk. Things that appear to be compromises to an individual artist may well be appropriate for the community. Sometimes a hymn or anthem you personally find offensive ought to be used. Further, the standards you use to judge the Chicago Symphony Orchestra are not appropriate to congregational singing. An offensive tone color or wrong pitch may be acceptable. A musician once told me he went to a church service and stopped singing so he could listen. "It sounded terrible," he said. Congregational singing may sound terrible when judged by professional standards because it is for participating, not for listening. Charles Ives' father George, a fine musician with perfect pitch, understood this need to suspend judgment. When someone asked him how he could stand to hear "old John Bell (. . . the best stonemason in town) bellow off-key," he replied,

> Old John is a supreme musician. Look into his face and hear the music of the ages. Don't pay too much attention to the sounds. If you do, you may miss the music.[4]

---

4. Henry and Sidney Lowell, *Charles Ives and His Music* (New York: Oxford University Press, 1955), 24.

On the other hand, compromising does not mean that any kind of musical slop in any unprepared state is acceptable. The highest possible artistic standards are applicable because God in Christ demands the best. It means choral standards, even when they cannot be reached, should be *higher* than those of the Robert Shaw Chorale or any other of the finest choral organizations you may imagine. It means the organist must prepare every hymn carefully. It means choosing worthy and durable music. God is present when Christ's body gathers, and you don't rush into the presence of the creator of the universe with ill-prepared—or well-prepared—trash. The task here is to understand the obvious tension between the perfection of God and the capacity of humanity. It is the most creative tension of all—the tension of the incarnation.

Fifth, as I just indicated, compromises are not necessarily bad. Good compromises can be creative and can lead to new life, like the incarnation. Having said that, however, there are also bad compromises. If you as the church musician are pushed around by a manipulative pastor, or, if one family in the church starts to control your choice of music, you have a bad compromise or no compromise at all. You cannot contribute your talents in such a situation because you are again reduced to being a music grinder or hired chattel. Even if you analyzed the fit as carefully as possible before you came, you may early or late discover that you did not analyze well enough. You may have to leave. You do not do this lightly, you do not do it without face-to-face discussions and meetings, and you do it with deep regret. But do it you must so that you can move to a place where serving the Lord and serving the people is possible.

This chapter is not about leaving, however. It is about beginning. Learn the story, develop your skills, look ahead realistically, find the best fit, and begin. Develop your craft by practicing it. You will soon be asking what your job really is. We must now address that issue, the heart of the matter.

Chapter 4

The Heart of the Matter

The Nature of the Church's Song

ASSUMING YOU HAVE FOUND A POSITION where the fit is right, what are you to do? What is your role? The question can be answered by looking first at the nature of the church's song. Five headings suggest themselves.

A Song of Praise

The church's song, especially for Protestants, is most obviously a song of praise. Many psalms—like 98, "O sing to the Lord a new song," or 100, which calls us to "come into [God's] presence with singing", or 150, where instruments and "everything that breathes" are all exhorted to praise the Lord—give expression to what is implicit throughout the Bible: God is to be praised, and music is one of the chief vehicles for expressing that praise.

Luther explains how this song of praise comes about.

> For God has cheered our hearts and minds through His dear Son, whom He gave for us to redeem us from sin, death, and the devil. He who believes this earnestly cannot be quiet about it. But he must gladly and willingly sing. . . .[1]

---

1. Martin Luther, "Preface to the Baptist Hymnal, 1545," *Luther's Works, Volume 53, Liturgy and Hymns*, Ulrich S. Leupold, ed. (Philadelphia: Fortress Press, 1965), 333.

God acts with loving-kindness toward us, and we respond with a jubilant song of praise. Praise is an essential part of the church's song from its most formal to its most informal expression.

Karl Barth, one of the most important twentieth century Reformed theologians, virtually made the church's song of praise a mark of the Christian community. He wrote,

> The praise of God which constitutes the community and its assemblies seeks to bind and commit and therefore to be expressed, to well up and be sung in concert. The Christian community sings. It is not a choral society. Its singing is not a concert. But from inner, material necessity it sings. . . .
>
> What we can and must say quite confidently is that the community which does not sing is not the community.[2]

A Song of Prayer

The song of the church is also a song of prayer. This perspective finds preeminent expression among Roman Catholics and those with more catholic liturgical forms. The roots of temple and synagogue worship are a sung tradition as are Christian liturgies of both the East and the West. Gregorian chant, which accompanied much of the Western liturgical tradition, is seen by some as prayer itself.[3] The Solesmes school of thought even calls Gregorian chant "a way of reaching up to God" and "a means of sanctification."[4]

While many who live in the heritage of the sixteenth century Reformers may wince at the Solesmes perspective because it can easily be seen as works' righteousness, John Calvin himself considered church song in the section on prayer in his *Institutes*,[5]

---

2. Karl Barth, *Church Dogmatics*, IV, Part Three, Second Half, trans. G.W. Bromiley (Edinburgh: T. & T. Clark), 866–867.

3. Dom Joseph Gajard, *The Solesmes Method*, trans. R. Cecile Gabain (Collegeville: The Liturgical Press, 1967), vii.

4. Ibid., 85.

5. John Calvin, *Institutes of the Christian Religion*, John T. McNeill, ed. (Philadelphia: Westminster Press, 1960), III, xx, 31–32.

Luther and the Lutheran Church retained the singing of collects
and indeed, the whole liturgy, and a large body of Protestant
hymns are in fact prayers. Though the emphasis may differ, almost all traditions treat music as prayer in some way. That
should not surprise us any more than using music as praise
should surprise us. Human beings both laugh and weep.
Laughter is the incipient form of sung praise, as weeping is the
incipient form of sung prayer.[6] The two often run into one another and cross.[7]

A Song of Proclamation

The church's song is also a song of proclamation. The author of
Ephesians expressed this by saying,

> be filled with the Spirit, as you sing psalms and
> hymns and spiritual songs. . . . (Eph. 5:18b-19a)

Here it is clear that music is a means by which the words and
word of the gospel are proclaimed. Luther referred to the parallel verse in Colossians (3:16) and wrote,

> St. Paul . . . exhorted the Colossians to sing spiritual
> songs and Psalms heartily unto the Lord so that God's
> word and Christian teaching might be instilled and
> implanted in many ways.[8]

An element of praise is often found in thoughts of this sort.
One can easily move from music as proclamation to music as
praise without realizing it. Such a leap removes the distinction
between these two motifs and tends to collapse one into the
other. Usually, since praise is so obvious, it takes precedence.

The use of music to proclaim the word, however, needs to
be kept separate, even though the connections to praise can be

---

6. Cf. Joseph Gelineau, *Voices and Instruments in Christian Worship* (Collegeville:
The Liturgical Press, 1964), 15–19.

7. For a helpful discussion of the primal nature and close relation of prayer and
praise, as well as their relation to thanksgiving and proclamation, see Patrick D.
Miller, Jr., *Interpreting the Psalms*, (Philadelphia: Fortress Press, 1986), 64–78.

8. Martin Luther, "Preface to the Wittenberg Hymnal, 1524," *Luther's Works*,
Vol. 53, 316.

close. This separation is needed not only for theological reasons, but to do justice to the church's musical heritage. Much of that heritage is exegetical or proclamatory: music helps to proclaim, to interpret, to break open the word of God. That is in part what happens when the congregation sings. That is why, from ancient times, Biblical lessons have been sung or chanted. Motets by Schütz and chorale preludes, cantatas, and Passions by Bach are more complex examples of the same intent. Without a *kerygmatic* (proclamatory) understanding of these pieces, they are incomprehensible.[9]

The Story

For many, praise, prayer, and proclamation move from the most to the least obvious definitions of church music. A still less obvious aspect of the church's song is, upon reflection, both the most obvious and the most profound: the church's song is story.

When the people of God recount the history of God's mighty acts, they invariably sing. The morning stars "sang together" at creation on behalf of the people (Job 38:7). After their deliverance from Egypt, Moses and the people sang a song (Exod. 25:1-8). The reason for the psalmists' songs of praise is that God "has done marvelous things" (Ps. 98:10). New Testament canticles such as the Magnificat (Luke 1:47-55) and the Benedictus (Luke 1:68-79) are songs recounting God's mighty deeds. The songs of Revelation tell the story of God's mighty acts in an eschatological frame of reference. From the beginning of the Biblical saga to its end, from one end of history to the other, the story is a song to be sung.

The same can be said of the church's hymnody. If you laid out the hymns of almost any mainstream hymnal in a sequential fashion, you would find the entire story of God's mighty acts there—from creation through Old Testament history to Christ's

---

9. See Robin A. Leaver, "The Liturgical Place and Homiletic Purpose of Bach's Cantatas," *Worship*, 59:3 (May, 1985), 194–202, and Robin A. Leaver, *J.S. Bach as Preacher: His Passions and Music in Worship* (St. Louis: Concordia Publishing House, 1984).

incarnation to church in the world "between the times," to last things. Individual hymns often tell the story by themselves. "Oh, Love, How Deep, How Broad, How High" is a good example. Music is the vehicle by which the community remembers and celebrates what God has done—which leads me to three points about the church's song as story.

First, it is sequentially and logically easy to lay out the story of the Bible from creation to consummation as I have just done in the last two paragraphs. In fact the story is more sophisticated than that, and sorting it out is more complicated. Like our own stories and those of the psalmist, it often begins in the midst of things with personal laments and personal songs of thanksgiving and with people who emerge on the stage of history with their own struggles and visions. For the Christian the event of Jesus stands at the center of the story and is its key. It radically alters and fulfills all personal laments, thanksgivings, struggles, and visions and gradually gives meaning to past and present.

Second, music has a peculiar communal and mnemonic character. A group who sings together becomes one and remembers its story, and therefore who it is, in a particularly potent way. Hitler knew and exploited the demonic potential of that reality. Whenever the church loses its song, a vacuum is created, which the Hitlers among us will invariably fill.

Third, music spins itself out through time just like the story which the song recounts and just like worship where the song is sung. As the Eastern Orthodox church knows so well, music "is by nature an event. It is dynamic rather than fixed." Like the story and like worship and "more than any other art . . . it carries the possibility of change, of transformation."[10] In other words, it is peculiarly suited not only to tell the story, but to accompany worship as well.

---

10. Archbishop John of Chicago, et al., *Sacred Music: Its Nature and Function* (Chicago: The Department of Liturgical Music, Orthodox Church in America, 1977), 2.

A Gift of God

Finally, the church's song, like music itself, is a gift of God. Music is a joy and delight with which God graces the creation. We do not bargain for it. We do not deserve it. It is simply freely given, there for the hearing, a joyous overflow of creation's goodness.

This gift can be viewed in many ways. One is the way Luther did it. Oskar Soehngen points out that Luther was forever amazed that music, this "unique gift of God's creation," comes from "the sphere of miraculous audible things,"[11] just like the word of God. This perceptive insight points to music as gift and to the close relationship between music and words: both are audible, words amazingly can be sung, and it is all gift.

A more Catholic approach, like Joseph Gelineau's, is to call music "God's daughter," given to humanity to signify the love of Christ. Viewed this way, music almost takes on the character of a sacramental sign that points beyond itself to pure love.[12] The Eastern Orthodox church often takes a similar view: music can "reflect the harmony of heaven" and "can provide us with a foretaste of the splendor of the Age to come."[13]

These views always bring with them music's power to uplift, transform, refresh, and recreate the heart and soul.[14] John Calvin asserts this view when he calls music a "gift of God deputed" for "recreating" humanity and giving us pleasure.[15] While Ulrich Zwingli in the sixteenth century related the refreshment of music to secular play, thereby giving music no relevance at all to worship,[16] even liberal Protestantism today may call music "rev-

11. Oskar Soehngen, "Fundamental Considerations for a Theology of Music," *The Musical Heritage of the Church*, vol. VI (St. Louis: Concordia Publishing House, 1962), 15.

12. Joseph Gelineau, *Voices and Instruments in Christian Worship* (Collegeville: The Liturgical Press, 1964), 27.

13. Archbishop John, 3.

14. Ibid., 2.

15. Charles Garside, Jr., "Calvin's Preface to the Psalter: A Re-Appraisal," *The Musical Quarterly* XXXVII (October 1951), 570.

16. See Charles Garside, Jr., *Zwingli and the Arts* (New Haven and London: Yale University Press, 1966).

elatory." Robert Shaw, for instance, when he was installed as Minister of Music of the First Unitarian Church of Cleveland, Ohio, quoted J. W. N. Sullivan, and argued that "a work of art may indeed be a 'revelation.'"[17] Many Christians would disagree with what Shaw means by revelation and worship, but his use of the term *revelation* shows how all worshiping traditions grapple with the gift of music and with its power.

The Cantor's Task

A host of theological issues attend these matters. The intent here is not to explain them in great detail. The point here is that defining the church's song under the headings of praise, prayer, proclamation, story, and gift offers clues to the dimensions of the cantor's task.

Leading the People's Praise

The cantor is the leader of the people's praise. The explosive response to God's grace, to be expressed, needs form and shape. Someone has to take responsibility for that forming and shaping, and this role belongs to the cantor. He or she has to sense the capacities and resources of a particular congregation, then write or choose music to express the praise of God with those capacities and resources. Once the music is composed and chosen, the cantor must then lead the people in actually singing the song of praise.

The song of praise is preeminently vocal. Words are the means by which our praise is articulated, and music is the means by which the articulation is carried aloft so that song gives wings to the words. But not only humanity sings this song of praise. The whole creation is called to join in. Instruments are therefore called to play their part. That part is not only to accompany the voices, but to sound alone where fitting and appropriate. The cantor is called to coordinate this mixture of vocal and instrumental music

17. Robert Shaw, "Music and Worship in the Liberal Church," *Typescript*, (September 25, 1967), 8.

and even play as talents warrant, so that instrumental music relates to the people's song of praise. Neither instrumental music nor any other music ought to be an afterthought or an unrelated addendum.

Leading the People's Prayer

The cantor aids the presiding or assisting minister in leading the people's prayer. The presiding and assisting ministers bear the primary responsibility for the proper prayers and petitions of a particular service, and the pastor bears the ultimate responsibility for the prayer life of a people. The cantor assists in this responsibility in the following ways.

First, the cantor provides the leadership for the people's litanic responses, spoken and sung. Corporate responses to a pastor's bids, even when spoken, are incipiently musical—elated forms of speech. The cantor through his or her direct leadership or through training of the choir shapes this response and thereby helps to shape the prayer life of the people.

Second, since some hymns are themselves prayers, the cantor sometimes leads the people in prayer by leading hymns. The choir also sings some texts that are prayers. In this case the cantor leads a group who prays on behalf of the people just as the pastor does. This act is obviously not a performance *before* the people; it is rather an act of intercession for and with the people.

Proclaiming the Word

The cantor aids the readers in the proclamatory work of reading lessons, which may on some occasions involve the use of more or less complex choral or solo settings of lessons in place of readings, rare for many of us. It should not be normative, although it deserves more consideration than we normally accord it. Where lessons are sung by a lector, the cantor should obviously aid those who do the singing. For most of us, lessons are read. There too the musician has a role we rarely think about, namely, helping readers read clearly. Musicians ought to understand phrasing and the ebb and flow of a line of words. Choral musicians ought to understand diction and enunciation. These skills are necessities in good reading which is close to a lost art in many churches and in the culture at large. Musicians can help repair the breach so that lessons can be understood.

The preacher obviously has the primary proclamatory task of publishing the good news of God's grace and love among us. By careful application to the Biblical word and the daily newspaper the preacher speaks his or her poor human words in the hope they will be heard as the Word of God itself so that the love of God in Christ will be known among us.

The cantor cannot and should not attempt to "preach" in the same way as the preacher because, first, the composing of text and music and the preparation of music by musicians preclude the preacher's relevance to the moment, and, second, the preacher can examine detailed relationships in spoken prose in a way that is not possible for the musician.

On the other hand, a polyphonic piece of music or the simultaneous juxtaposition of two texts gives the musician an opportunity to proclaim relationships in a way that is not open to the preacher, who must communicate in a stream of monologue. And, while the relevance of the moment is not the responsibility of music, which is of necessity more prepared and formal, music has the capacity for breaking open a text in a way spoken words cannot do. In singing a hymn or hearing a Schütz motet or a Bach cantata, many Christians have shared William Cowper's experience.

> Sometimes a light surprises
> The Christian while he sings;
> It is the Lord who rises
> With healing in his wings.[18]

Telling the Story

The cantor helps the people sing the whole story and thereby tells the story. The preacher also tells the story, of course, as does

---

18. This text by William Cowper (1731–1800), while it requires inclusivising, nonetheless points to a recurrent experience of the Christian church at song.

the teacher. Some understandings of preaching would even argue that it is at heart story-telling: proclaiming the good news is telling the story of God's love. But the preacher is always compelled to apply the story to us in this moment so that the searing edge of God's love can burn its way into our hearts. It requires the context of the whole story, and preaching can only give that context over time or in an ancillary way. The cantor is responsible for the context and the fullness of the story.

The cantor tells the story by seeing to it that the whole story is sung. The lessons, prayers, and sermon for a given service are likely to have a thematic focus. The hymnody, psalmody, and anthems ought to relate to that focus also, but in addition they flesh out the rest of the story and remind us of other parts of the plot. Over the course of a year the whole story should certainly have been sung, from creation to last things. In other words, doing the same six or ten hymns over and over does not serve the people well, because it keeps them from singing the whole story and omits much of the context the preacher needs for his or her words.

Music is related not simply to the story, but to time. This element gives the musician a peculiar and remarkable responsibility. The church musician tells time for the people, which is, in part, true in the way I have described singing the story. But in part it is true in direct relation to a service of worship, since music spins itself out in time just as worship does. Music accompanies processions, either of all the people or of some of the people for everyone else. This processional nature of the pilgrim people on the move takes place in time. Music that accompanies processions articulates that time. Beyond that, music articulates worship itself. That is, the church musician is the one who controls the shape and flow of a service more than anyone else. Points of beginning and ending—an entrance rite, for example, or the reading of lessons followed by sermon and hymn, or receiving holy communion—almost invariably have musical components that accompany them, including silence which is music's backdrop. The sensitive church musician handles this responsibility with great care and a tremendous sense of concern for the people.

The Steward of God's Gift

The cantor is the steward of God's gracious gift of music. Since this gift is so powerful, the steward receives tremendous power as the deputy. The power can easily be misused for selfish ends of ego gratification and personal power. The cantor is called therefore to the paradox of using the power granted, but of using it with restraint on behalf of God in Christ from whom all blessings—including this one—flow.

That paradox brings with it another. The cantor knows that the preacher or lector can stumble over a word here or there, and still the message will have its impact. To stumble over a note is much more dangerous. The impact will dissipate much more quickly when there is a musical error. So the cantor is constantly constrained to achieve an excellence and perfection which is ultimately never humanly possible. The need for excellence drives the church musician to rehearse and practice every detail until it is right, for without practice the necessary perfection and excellence will certainly never be achieved. The paradox is that even with disciplined rehearsing, we have no guarantee. The musician who is at all sensitive knows that when she or he finally gets it right, that too is a gift for which the only appropriate response is thanksgiving.

Approaching the Task

Having determined what to do is not quite enough. Three further components of the cantor's role need to be articulated. They fit under the heading of how to approach the task.

First, the cantor is serving a specific people. As I indicated earlier, your responsibility as cantor is to allow the song of the people of God in your place to find expression. You do that not by superimposing an unattainable ideal and then flagellating yourself and your parish for never reaching it. The ideal relates to the people and choir and musicians you have to work with because God is present among them with the song. Your responsibility is to allow that song to find expression, which is ultimately the ideal.

This broad goal does not suggest that there are no standards. Certain standards exist for music just as the ten commandments are standards for living. The church as a community of grace, however, begins with grace, not with the law. So the cantor begins with God's gracious gift of music among a given people, not with arbitrary legal constructs and rules of constraint. The incipient song must find expression. Essentially, this means selecting durable music worth the people's time and effort, then doing things musically so that the people are invited to sing. The examples of a beautifully-shaped phrase, organ playing that breathes with the people, rhythm that pulsates, and melodies that sing all will do more to give the song expression than heavy-handed rules and legalistic constraints. Any musical person knows this almost instinctively.

Second, the cantor's craft must be exercised with kindness and compassion. Many musicians in our culture get by with being temperamental because we somehow believe that artists are naturally temperamental and should be humored. This behavior is especially true of some secular instrumental and choral conductors, who regularly throw temper tantrums and treat people poorly to achieve their ends.

Temperamental conductors have in the past, and to a certain extent still today, virtually become an accepted cultural reality for musicians and the general public, and church musicians have often felt compelled to imitate their example. The cantor knows another reality—that all people are to be treated with respect because they are loved by God. Music is for people. People are not for music. Nobody has the right to treat other human beings poorly.

This admonition is not to suggest that cantors can be more perfect than any other group of people. Like all musicians and all people, they will sometimes get angry, lose their tempers, and be temperamental. This is to suggest that the ideal is kindness and compassion and that we gather around the song God gives us, not around the personality of the conductor.

Third, a word needs to be said specifically about leadership of the song. It is a complex matter and needs great sensitivity. At certain times, such as Easter Sunday morning on an explosive hymn of resurrection joy, the organ can appropriately drive the congregation with a powerful rhythmic punch. Generally the organ should lead—sensitively, but lead. At other times, however, such as the singing of responsorial psalms or prayers, neither organ nor conducting seems appropriate, as the community finds its own tempo with only a breath from the cantor to set things in motion. I once heard George Black—one of the past presidents of the Hymn Society in the United States and Canada, and former professor of French and Church Music at Huron College, University of Western Ontario—say that a community of love will sing together, that to tamper with the people's prayer is a tricky business, and that the cantor needs faithfully to take some risks, like sometimes letting the people set their own tempo. Cantors need to ponder those profoundly true observations in their hearts and experience them with their communities of faith. Church musicians ought not always to conduct nor overtly control everything with the voice or organ or other instruments. Tight control is not leadership. It is more an exhibition of our own problems, our own insecurities, and our unwillingness to allow the people's voice to find expression.

Leadership, then, involves a balance of many items. The style of music (a rhythmic chorale from the sixteenth century has a different "ideal" tempo than a nineteenth century tune), the nature of the text, the place in the service, the time of year, the time of day, the weather, the size and acoustics of the building, the tradition of the congregation, the nature of the community (young or old, good or ill health), the size of the community, the pacing of the pastor, and your own tendencies are among the things you need to consider. They need thoughtful attention prior to the service, but you also must respond in the moment to the event of music-making itself. Wonderful surprises can happen if you are sensitive and simply allow them to occur. Charismatic communities sometimes know this best, but the Holy Spirit graces all our worship and leads us all into ever new truths.

Chapter 5

The Rhythm of the Cantor's Life

Sunday

The Christian church has designated Sunday in various ways. It is the day of resurrection, when the boundaries of time and space were shattered by Christ's rising from the dead. Each Sunday is a little Easter. It is the day when Christ meets his people eucharistically, breaking bread with his disciples (as in Luke 24:30) and with the whole church thereafter. It is the first day of the week, the day of creation, of divine initiatives, and of the new age. It is also the eighth day, the day when Christ breaks out of time and history into his kingdom and lifts humanity into an eternal dimension. It is the Lord's day, the day on which Christ appears in glory and indicates the end-time has begun, the day when Christ manifests his messianic powers.[1]

All these designations point to the importance of Sunday for Christians and explain why Sunday has been the traditional day of Christian assembly for worship. Like the life of the church itself, so the life of the cantor revolves around Sunday.

---

1. For a description of the Sabbath and Sunday, see Therry Maertens, *A Feast in Honor of Yahweh*, trans. Kathryn Sullivan (Notre Dame: Fides Publishers, Inc., 1965), 152–192.

45

As the first day of the week, Sunday initiates the week's beginning. It is the day from which all other days take their meaning, the day from which all other days spin off. The Christian counts one plus six, and the banquet on the one nourishes the body of Christ to be that healing body in the world for the other six.

The church musician as Christian also counts one plus six. But the church musician as church musician is always preparing for the weekly banquet. The cantor is called like the clergy to prepare the feast on behalf of the host and the people. Therefore, the cantor as cantor looks forward to Sunday as a chef and waiters look forward to the banquets they prepare.

Preparation

The cantor or cantorial staff has to work with two levels of preparation. One is for the immediate Sunday that is coming. The other is for Sundays in advance, preferably three months to a year or more. Preparation for the immediate Sunday is obviously most detailed. Preparation for more distant Sundays becomes increasingly more general as it extends farther into the future.

Tasks

In any given week the two levels of preparation lead to the following tasks for the cantor:

- Meeting with the pastor
- Meeting with the worship and music committee or some other committee or planning group
- Planning music
- Composing and arranging music
- Practicing
- Rehearsing with choirs, soloists, instrumentalists, or anyone else for whom the cantor is responsible (readers, in some cases)
- Spending social time with people of the parish

The cantor's role as teacher leads to several other related responsibilities, namely,

- Preparing classes
- Teaching them
- Writing for parish publications like monthly newsletters

These ten tasks do not necessarily all happen each week, and they vary from parish to parish and from person to person in their presence and intensity. To get a sense of this variability, let us construct examples of small, moderate, and large churches, then refer to these examples in discussing the cantor's tasks.

A small church might take several forms. In one, perhaps forty to eighty people come to worship each Sunday; there is a small organ; the choir has seven members not distributed very well among the sections; the pastor is part-time; and the budget and resources are limited. This church might be stable in its size, or it may be in the process of growth. In either case, it could have a relatively vigorous congregational life, though the former is likely to be less active. Another small possibility is a house church with fewer than twenty-five people, no choir and no building to keep up, but a vigorous and committed life together. Yet another congregation might have a large building and sixty older people left from a time when the congregation numbered in the hundreds. Most of the people have now moved away or have died, and a large building with a pipe organ and part-time pastor remain. These three churches are different, yet they share a small size.

For the moderate-sized church, let's take a congregation of six hundred people or so on its rolls, of whom somewhere between one and two hundred attend worship each Sunday. The choir might number twelve to twenty people and approximate some balance; or at least all sections are represented. This congregation might have more than one service on Sunday, though only one is just as likely. It could have a budget for music and musicians, a full-time pastor, and some musical resources like an organ, piano, handbells, choral library, and even a rehearsal room. The organ and piano might be poor, but they might also be of excellent quality. This church will probably always feel it has to struggle, but it has the staff, the resources, and the flexibility to do many things.

For the large church, picture two thousand members or more, several full-time staff members including at least one musician, several services each Sunday and at other times, multiple choirs, various instrumental groups, an extensive music library, a fine organ, many educational and other programs for all ages, a large budget, perhaps a concert series, and resources that make possible large expenditures at regular intervals.

Meeting With the Pastor

In any of these churches, a healthy cantorial role begins with a healthy relationship between the pastor (or priest or minister—choose your favorite term) and the church musician. Weekly meetings or contact of some sort with the pastor are therefore crucial. In the small church these may happen by telephone or informally. In the larger church they may be structured into weekly staff meetings. No one prescription holds for every situation, but some general guidelines are appropriate.

First, the clergy-cantor relationship is a powerful partnership, which begins by working at worship on behalf of the people. In chapter 8 this subject is discussed more fully with examples of nonpartnerships, so it is sufficient simply to mention it here.

Second, the clergy and cantor have to work out a system of planning for the immediate Sunday and for successive Sundays so that the two work as a team. They must have an understanding of who does what, when it is to be done, and how what they do fits together at a given service. Who chooses hymns? When? When is the sermon topic decided? When does the musician know the topic? Is there a common understanding of the character the lessons and prayers impart to a given Sunday? When is that discussed so appropriate music can be selected far enough in advance to prepare adequately? The schizoid condition of much American worship results from a failure of clergy and cantor to ask or resolve many of these and other related questions.

Third, clergy and cantor need not agree about everything, but they must come to an understanding about what they are doing in worship and why. This task requires weekly communication of some sort, no matter how brief (or how lengthy—communication cannot be measured by minutes in a meeting).

Fourth, cantor and clergy need to be "pastor" to one another at times, that is, to listen sensitively to the other's joys and sorrows. While church leaders are expected to do this with the congregation, they often forget that they owe it to one another.

Lastly, in parishes with weekly staff meetings, staff members may find benefit in sharing and knowing about common problems in order to get a perspective on the life of the whole church. But it is pointless to waste the cantor's time with all the minister's problems or to waste the minister's time with all the cantor's problems. Needless meetings are as onerous as no meetings at all.

Meeting With Committees

In the small church, especially the house church, committee meetings may consist of the church meeting as a committee of the whole, as necessary, before or after worship. Some small committee meetings may of course still occur from time to time. In the large church, a number of more structured meetings typically take place each week. For these the cantor must either prepare agendas or make responses, then coordinate musical activities in the parish so that some overall coherence is always achieved. For the moderate-sized parish, weekly to monthly meetings is more likely to be the norm with fewer things to coordinate.

Planning Music

The cantor's first concern is the people's song. The people sing four things: the Ordinary of the liturgy (or, in some traditions, recurrent pieces like the "Gloria Patri"), the psalmody (still spoken in some places, but often, sung as is its normative and original character), responsorial forms of prayer, and hymns. In any size parish all these things have to be planned.

I do not mean "choosing" the hymns. That task is presumed. Planning music begins after the hymns are selected. I have in mind here how the liturgy and hymns will be introduced, what setting of the liturgy and hymns will be used, how the psalms will be sung, who will sing which stanzas of the hymns (men, women, the choir, all?), how they will be sung (in canon, in parts, in unison?), which instruments will join the singing or play alone for one stanza or on introductions, whether the choir will sing the Propers, whether they will sing part of the Ordinary on the people's behalf, what forms of prayer will be used, and related questions.

Decisions about these matters need to relate to substance, not arbitrary whims. For instance, the Hebrew parallelism of some psalms can sometimes be expressed by alternating groups. If a psalm has a built-in refrain, like verses 4, 8, and 12 of Psalm 46 in some versions, the people can sing the refrain and a soloist can sing the other verses. Stanzas of hymns can be accompanied in such a way that the one most closely related to the pastor's sermon stands out. Alternation can achieve this, or can be done purely for variety, especially on long hymns, to help invigorate hymn singing.

Much of this detailed planning may seem subtle. It is. But people will be influenced positively, glean new insights, and worship with more integrity, even if they are not consciously aware of the planning you have done. Others will be aware of what is happening and will be openly appreciative. The more you plan in this way, the more their numbers will increase—and so will the people's song.

For an informal house church much of this planning can happen before or at the worship service itself, as the whole body functions virtually as the cantorial staff. Even there, however, someone invariably exerts a leadership role, and some future planning is always necessary if only because hymnic, psalmodic, and liturgical materials (such as hymnals or sheets with proper copyright permissions) have to be supplied. If a piano, harpsichord, guitar, or other instrument or instrumental group is to be used, a whole new range of planning responsibilities is introduced.

This other range of responsibilities comes with the cantor's territory in the usual parish. The responsibilities become increasingly numerous and complex the larger the parish. More instruments, a larger organ, more choirs, more services, and a larger worshiping congregation lead to more resources and more possibilities for praise, prayer, proclamation, and varied ways to sing the story. These opportunities also can lead to less and less participation by the people until the central thing—the people's song—is silent, and choirs and instruments always do it for the people by proxy. This silencing of the people is the ever-present temptation of the large parish, and the cantor's planning has to guard against it.

I do not mean to suggest that the large parish should cancel concert series and obliterate choral or organ programs. Of course the church should support these, and, of course, they too need to be carefully planned. The finest choirs in the world are church choirs, and choral music and organ music are the church's birthright—worthy of fullest support. Some parishes have a special responsibility for concert series or for choral services. The whole church needs to treasure them. They are not the norm, however, and even for them the choral and organ planning needs to grow out of the worship life of the people and out of the people's song, not be arbitrarily superimposed. The lessons, verses, and prayers for a given Sunday ought to generate the hymns, choral, organ, and other instrumental music. To reverse this order is to skew the priorities. It also means the amateur seven-member choir in the small parish is as important as the choirboys at Westminster Abbey. Even a choir of two or three can lead the singing. It can prepare stanzas of hymns alone. It can sing Proper sentences at the lessons or the offertory or communion. Small choirs may sing mostly unison or two-part music. That's fine. The choir with the requisite resources should sing the Bach cantatas. Every parish is not constrained to sing them or to produce the choral delights of St. Olaf College or Westminster Choir

College. A singing parish, not choral perfection, is the ideal for the normal church.

The second priority for planning relates to choirs and instruments singing or playing alone, but always in connection with the liturgy, hymns, psalmody, and prayers. Choirs, organ, or instruments can sing or play stanzas of hymns by themselves. Where the resources are available, cantatas and anthems for choral and instrumental forces of all sizes and abilities should be chosen, provided they relate to the lessons, prayers, and sermon topic of the day. All of these elements need to be planned well enough in advance so musicians can be prepared.

Finally, preludes, voluntaries, and postludes need to be chosen. Note that they are last in planning, as they are least in importance. They can be built on hymns, relate to melodic materials or keys of hymns or other service music, or reflect the style or mood of a given service. These elements need careful long-range planning, for they have value in mirroring, heightening, or introducing the jubilation or mourning of a given day. But they are not the central thing, and to plan only them at the expense of planning the more central service music is to focus on what is at best tertiary. They may be omitted, and the worship's integrity is in no way threatened. The small parish with the small electronic organ that is about to die may even choose to omit separate organ music altogether and thereby achieve a positive gain rather than a loss.

Composing Music

Not all cantors are composers, and a cantor does not have to compose to do the job well. Church musicians often feel they ought not to compose, however, which is a mistake. We still live in the backwaters of a late nineteenth-century misconception that regards composers as super-human geniuses, separated from the rest of us by an impassable chasm. The corollary of this nonsense is that we poor mortals have no business composing at all, because to do less than to compose for eternity is a sacrilege, and only the super-human genius composes for eternity.

The cantor and parish must abandon this foolishness and see things as they are. Composing for eternity is not necessary. Composing for now will do nicely. It's enough. *Gebrauchsmusik*, functional music for the occasion, has a proud history. Nobody knows better than the cantor what the people in a specific place need. And nobody can supply the need better than the cantor.

To compose is literally "to place" (Latin, *poser*) "together" (*com*). Planning is already placing music together. Writing music simply carries this planning one step farther. Almost any musician has creative compositional urges, and these urges can be channeled. Composition is a craft, which can be learned and practiced. It is not a mysterious mystique dwelling in some shrouded mist. Every musician will not be Palestrina or Bach, or Beethoven or Stravinsky, to be sure. But their genius is not required.

It is perfectly appropriate for the cantor to compose a refrain, a hymn tune, a hymn introduction, a harmonization, or an anthem—even a hymn text—that fits as precisely as possible the need of a given occasion. You may require a refrain related to a certain hymn tune. Compose it. It may take much time and effort. Do it only if you are willing to work at it with care. The congregation does not deserve ill-conceived and hurriedly assembled trash. They deserve the best, and, if you work at it, you can provide what is best precisely for their situation.

For anyone who is *driven* to compose, the cantorial post offers a remarkable array of possibilities—from the simplest congregational refrains to the most complex polytonal choral or instrumental pieces. Service music, organ music, solos, hymn tunes, hymn concertatos, and many arrangements all cry out to be written for specific times and places. The cantor who writes them can actually use them. Don Mead, a fine Chicago area cellist and organist who plays for First Congregational Church in Glen Ellyn, Illinois, once told me he liked the church position because he knew of no other musical post where the musician's creativity could find so much expression. He is right.

Practicing

Time must be set aside each week to practice on the two levels of preparation—for the immediate Sunday and for the future. Without practice, planning is pointless. I am not talking here about practicing for concerts, though cantors who are also concert artists will practice for both activities and find that one helps the other. I have in mind here practicing for the people's song.

For the organist this means working out introductions, practicing each stanza of every hymn (you cannot know a hymn too well), practicing anthems and all the other service music, and carefully working out registrations. For the vocalist who alternates with the congregation or leads it, it means vocalizing and preparing what needs to be sung just as one would practice for a solo recital.

In some situations, like the house church where you may only set the pitch, practicing may not require much time. In large churches where you have a large organ that leads all the hymns, many hours may be spent each week practicing hymn settings. The small parish with the large church building and organ may imply many hours of organ practice. The small parish with the inadequate organ may, paradoxically, demand long hours of practice to make the instrument sound as good as it can. This kind of practice is not terribly satisfying, but it must be done.

A word is in order here about varying accompaniments to hymns. The Calvinist, or Reformed, heritage originally permitted only *a cappella* psalm singing in unison without instrumental accompaniment or polyphony of any kind. Presbyterians, Congregationalists, and other Reformed groups have by now generally adopted hymns, organs, additional instruments as needed, and harmonized hymn settings, but they have often translated the old Reformed stricture against instruments and polyphony into a new one (usually unwritten) against altered harmonizations.[2] My own view is that this new stricture, like the

2. See, for example, Robert Baker, "The Organist's Role in Public Worship," *Reformed Liturgy & Music*, xviii:4 (Fall 1984), 167–169.

old one, limits or even precludes the exegetical role of the organist or the choral or instrumental director and does not necessarily aid the congregation's singing. Each person must decide this issue based on her or his own theology of music and must work it out with a given parish within its theology and practice. I do not mean to argue the point here; I want to say only that the Reformed stricture does *not* mean no practice is required. Even where little or no variation occurs from stanza to stanza, hymns must be practiced. Phrasing, articulation, tempo, cadences, pauses for breathing and swallowing between stanzas, musical and stylistic playing and singing, and—for the organist—registrations, pedaling, fingering, all need to be worked out, whether harmonizations are varied or not. The people's singing depends on it. And that is the cantor's fundamental responsibility.

Rehearsing With Others

The cantor has some control over his or her own private practice time. Practice can be lengthened or shortened and can be early in the morning or late at night, if necessary. Rehearsals with others are more restricted both in the *amount* of time available and *when* the time is available.

The cantor has to arrange rehearsals in advance. Letters, postcards, phone calls, and reminders are all necessary, and time must be allotted for them. Arrangements with musicians who come in for special occasions, like instrumentalists, are especially important. These people will not know the schedule the way a church choir does. They need to know times for rehearsals and services, and they need to know how much you will pay them, if they are being paid.

Rehearsals must be carefully prepared. Here the two levels of planning are most obvious. Music for the coming Sunday has to be polished, and music for the future has to be started or continued. It is best to plan far ahead for the choir—at least four weeks, preferably eight weeks or a season or even a year or more for an especially complex piece—so that they can learn the music. The cantor needs to know the choir's capabilities and to build in enough repetition so that sickness or other unavoidable absences will not lessen the end result.

Rehearsal time is extremely precious. There is never enough of it. The cantor must guard it ferociously. Rehearsals need to begin and end precisely as promised, and between those limits the time has to be used as efficiently as possible to accomplish as much as possible. Accomplishing such a goal requires careful prior planning and then a capacity to switch from plan A to plan B or to improvise yet another plan when you get to the rehearsal and discover that all the sopranos are home with the flu.

Instrumentalists who come to play for services are not likely to understand hymn singing or the singing of the liturgy. Their playing in these connections has to be carefully rehearsed, more carefully than preludes or voluntaries. The cantor needs to allot adequate time for this rehearsing.

The cantor has to make certain that all rehearsing prepares for leading the people in song. In other words, the demands of the liturgy, hymnody, psalmody, prayer, and everything connected with them are the first priority. Then come the Propers or anthems the choir may sing alone or preludes and voluntaries instrumentalists may play alone. These elements also need to be carefully prepared and related to the specific Sunday.

Social Time With the People

The cantor's role in leading the congregation's song places the cantor close to the people. In a sense the cantor is the congregation. When the cantor breathes (at the organ or with the voice), the people breathe. When the cantor changes the articulation or shapes a phrase well, the people follow. When the cantor changes the loudness or timbre, the volume and color of the people's singing changes.

Therefore, the cantor must know the people, which means spending time with them. A cantor can invest this time both profitably and enjoyably at coffee hours, before or after meetings, at social gatherings, in phone conversations or visits, or in other ways. The people need to be able to speak freely and openly to the cantor and the cantor freely and openly to them. Without this exchange the cantor leads the song in a vacuum.

Time must be allotted for this, but not all the time. As some church musicians avoid it altogether, so some spend all their time socializing. Neither extreme is desirable. If socializing starts to eat up practice time, something is wrong. A balance is not dificult to achieve if one is conscious about achieving it.

Preparing and Teaching Classes

In some small church situations, the cantor will have virtually no teaching responsibilities other than teaching music to the choir and congregation. In some large churches virtually every week may be filled with classes to teach. In moderate-sized parishes, the situation may vary from week to week, month to month, and year to year.

In all teaching situations the cantor simply has to be the best possible teacher, which means researching and knowing material well, planning class sessions carefully, then lecturing or leading discussions as a good teacher would. Time obviously has to be allotted for the preparation as well as for the teaching itself. Careful preparation is especially critical the shorter the teaching time. For instance, three minutes to teach the congregation a part of the liturgy or a new hymn before the service must be skillfully prepared so that the learning takes place and not an instant is wasted.

Writing for Parish Publications

If a monthly newsletter goes out to the congregation, the cantor may find it useful to have a column in it. Many things—from practical matters to hymn studies to theological or musical explanations—can be shared. Some cantors use Sunday bulletins to write briefly, several lines or less, about one hymn. It helps the cantor's teaching function.[3]

---

3. For some fine examples, which can be used just as they are, see Austin Lovelace, *Hymn Notes for Church Bulletins* (Chicago: G. I. A. Publications, 1987).

A large parish may provide many possibilities for the cantor to write for the congregation. The small parish may have few. Whenever there are regular written publications, however, the cantor should have some space, no matter how brief, in them. And it should be filled with meaning, not froth. Communicating in this way means time for preparation. Ideas for writing (and for rehearsals and services and meetings, etc.) can be refined as you drive back and forth to church.

A Week in the Cantor's Life

Let us assume now that the cantor plays the organ, directs the choirs, and handles all the musical responsibilities of the church. If you wish to assume a division of labor (one person plays the organ, another directs one choir, etc.), split up the following for your own needs.

The cantor's week in the small church might look like this: on Sunday morning the cantor checks with the pastor about last minute details at 8:00 A.M., has a rehearsal with the choir from 8:30 to 9:45, begins the prelude a few minutes before 10:00, plays and directs the music of the service from 10:00 to 11:00, spends some time with the people until 11:30, and checks with the minister about future planning before leaving at 12:00. During the week several phone conversations with the pastor, members of the choir, and perhaps some parishioners take place; final decisions are made about next week's worship, and the information is given to the secretary for the bulletin; some future planning is done for a half hour or so at home; and, if the church is not too far, practice is possible on the organ for a couple of days, and some things can be worked out at home on the piano, especially score study. On Saturday, an hour or two of practice and rehearsal preparation for Sunday takes place. Most of the week's activity for this cantor involves four hours on Sunday. Perhaps ten to twelve hours a week (including Sunday) are required.

In the moderate-sized parish the cantor can anticipate a meeting with the pastor during the week, a meeting with a committee, at least one choir rehearsal on a weekday night and maybe another rehearsal at some other time if there is a youth or bell choir, time for phone calls, time for getting Sunday's music ready for the secretary to list in the service leaflet, time for future planning, and daily practice and score study if at all possible. On Saturday a couple of hours of practice must be done just for Sunday. On Sunday the cantor will arrive early enough to see the pastor and practice briefly before the choir rehearsal at 9:30, which ends in time for the prelude just before 10:00. The service goes from 10:00 to 11:00 (or there might be two services), and time can be spent with the people after the service/s. Since more happens during the week here, less is packed into Sunday morning than in the small church. Seeing the pastor after the service is not so necessary, for example. This job will take a minimum of fifteen to twenty hours a week and maybe twenty-five or more.

In either of the two previous examples, teaching could be included. In the large church it almost certainly will be. The cantor's week in the large church is generally filled with activities as follows: Daily practice and some study must be protected. They will all too easily be eaten away by correspondence, planning, phone calls, staff meetings, socializing, housekeeping details, rehearsal, and class preparation—all of which has to be organized into a daily or weekly schedule of some sort. Rehearsals themselves might look something like this: junior high choir after school on Tuesday, younger children after school on Wednesday, adults on Thursday evening, senior high choir on Sunday evening, and a bell choir or choirs at various other times of one or several days. Each week will almost certainly include a class or students to teach, committee meetings, and a dinner or two. Sunday morning will likely involve at least three morning services with a rehearsal before each one and perhaps a Sunday afternoon service with a rehearsal before that one also. Services on Saturday and at other times are also possible. This job will take a minimum of forty hours a week and will include more to do no matter how much time is spent at it.

A Year in the Cantor's Life

In the early church a festival recalling Christ's death and resurrection was celebrated each year. Gradually it was refracted into Holy Week and Lent prior to Easter, and Pentecost after it. Eventually a second cycle developed around the birth of Christ.

Except for those who retain Puritan scruples about celebrating Christmas, most churches today organize their yearly life around the two cycles of Christmas and Easter. This practice provides a way of sanctifying time, of living through the events we remember, and of teaching and recalling the major themes of the faith. For the cantor the church year and the three-year ecumenical lectionary, which many denominations have now adopted, are especially significant because they tell the whole story. Since the cantor is responsible for the whole story, the church year and lectionary are among the cantor's most valuable allies. They guard against individual biases and help us remember parts of the story we find less palatable or more difficult while at the same time they prevent us from riding our own hobbies.

Advent provides four weeks of preparation for both the first and final coming of Christ. Christmas celebrates the incarnation as Advent's fulfillment and a conclusion derived from Easter. Epiphany bridges the birth and Passion of Jesus. Lent is a forty-day period of instruction and discipleship for Christians and those who are to be baptized at the Easter Vigil, which culminates in remembering Christ's crucifixion. It is followed by the joyful celebration of God's victory over sin and death at Easter, which in turn is followed by a fifty-day period of jubilation. The jubilation culminates in Pentecost when the birthday of the church is recalled. A series of Sundays after Pentecost reaches through the summer and fall (in our hemisphere) to the beginning of Advent, when the cycle begins anew near the first part of December.

The rhythm of the church's year dictates the rhythm of the cantor's year. At Christmas, and especially as Lent nears Easter, there will be more rehearsals and services. Choirs and faithful parishioners often speak of pitching tents at the church for the central week called Holy Week and especially the "Three Days"

(Triduum) of Maundy Thursday, Good Friday, and Easter Vigil on Saturday.

Obviously just prior to and at these peak periods meetings become fewer while practicing, rehearsing, and services themselves increase immensely. The cantor's usual number of hours per week may easily double. On the other hand, during Sundays after Pentecost when choirs are often on vacation, activities decrease greatly so that fewer hours than normal balance the festival increases. It is often a good idea to spend more time for one or two of the quiet summer weeks planning the entire next year and ordering music. This tactic lightens the planning load when rehearsals and other activities are at partial or full tilt.

Weddings and Funerals

Weddings and funerals are part of the church musician's occasional responsibilities. For some large churches they may become more normative than occasional. They can be unusually meaningful occasions or terribly demoralizing ones.

People often use and abuse the church for weddings. With no relation to or understanding of the church or marriage, they want the trappings of a church wedding without its essence. They want embarrassingly trivial music, a movie scene that does not translate into real life, a public bedroom, or a sentimental journey that leads nowhere. A prominent organist once told me he finally recommended to such people that they go to the local funeral parlor and let the funeral director turn it into a wedding parlor for them. Many times cantors feel like saying that, and sometimes they probably should, but the pastoral role of the cantor also needs to be remembered. Weddings are occasions for teaching people what the church and marriage are really about.

Funerals, especially those at funeral parlors, can be sentimental attempts to avoid death's icy finality, but funerals in church are generally more positive. People there seem much more honest, willing to face death in the context of Christ's victory over it, and able to grieve mournfully and ultimately with resurrection joy. Such occasions are profoundly powerful, as are sensible weddings.

The cantor needs to remember and to remind people that weddings and funerals are first of all services of worship. Prayers, lessons, sermons, the Lord's Supper, hymn-singing, and psalm-singing are not only possible; they are implicit. The people have a song to sing at these occasions, maybe especially at these occasions. It cries out to be sung. The cantor has to help the people express it. When it finds expression, new life in Christ is revealed in a singularly powerful way.

Weddings and funerals are essentially congregational events. Congregations need to work out with pastors and cantors what ministry means on these occasions and how the congregation expects the pastor and cantor to give leadership in this ministry. This policy can be articulated in a brochure or statement to be shared with the whole congregation and with anyone who requests a wedding or funeral. When it is done in this way, the perspective is clear, the congregation's integrity is maintained, nobody is cast in the role of a spoiler, and the church indeed carries out its ministry.

The "policy" then translates into time for congregational meetings and educational sessions, time for meeting with brides and grooms and, occasionally, time for meeting with the bereaved. For some weddings, considerable rehearsal and meeting time is required. For funerals there is often little chance for practice, so it is well to have appropriate music prepared and in one's repertoire. Finally, of course, time must be allotted for the services themselves and sometimes for meals or receptions that follow them.

Time and Vocation

This chapter has been about time and vocation. It indicates the way the role of the cantor works itself out. It explains how the cantor uses time, and what she or he is called to do in that time. The right use of time and a proper sense of vocation for the cantor in the small, moderate, or large church always have the same heart, center, and goal: the people's song.

Chapter 6

Measuring Gain and Growth

To what does the cantor aspire? How do you measure it?

The cantor aspires to become less and less obvious. The task is to enable the people to sing. The better the cantor does his or her job, the more the people sing. The more the people sing, the less they seem to depend upon the cantor. Paradoxically, the cantor, like the good teacher, aspires to become transparent. Or, to say the same thing another way, the cantor aspires to lead the song in such a way that the song itself takes over, and leadership becomes hidden within the song.

How do you measure that process? You don't do it by first establishing behavioral objectives or making statistical tabulations that measure decibels or intonation or pitch or rhythm or numbers in the choir or anything else—a clever way of pretending to evaluate while actually hiding from the evaluation itself. You do it by first asking, "Are the people singing the Lord's song?"

There are two parts to that question. The second part, the Lord's song, can be measured easily. Simply look to see if all the parts of the story are there. Is the full range of your hymnic heritage being employed, or are you singing the same ten hymns over and over again? Is the whole story there—creation and Old Testament roots, the birth, life, passion, death, and resurrection of Christ, the church's story, individual redemption, contemporary society's ethical concerns, and final consummation? Or are you stuck only in the warmth of personal conversion or sentimental escape or one ethical issue or Lent all year? Your tradition will have its own characteristic musical style, but the cantor is responsible to work out from that central style to other styles, thereby filling out the story with other musical manifestations of it and keeping the parish aware both of its own specific heritage and of the catholicity of the whole church past and present. One of the most dangerous temptations of contemporary Christians is to assume that they are the first and only Christians who ever lived and that their style is the only one. The cantor especially knows another reality and must always keep the church aware of it. Are you and your church stuck in one style and one style only? Establish your own grid of questions, keep track of the hymns, psalms, and anthems you sing, and ask whether your choices reflect the emphases of the seasons, the lectionary, the whole story. Gaps that need to be filled will quickly become obvious.

Another way to ask this half of the question is to see if praise, prayer, proclamation, story, and music as gift are present. Does your church sing its praise, prayer, proclamation, and story, and is it graced with the gift of music?

To ask the question this way requires looking at your resources. The question here is not only whether texts of praise, prayer, proclamation, story, and gift are being sung, though that is part of it. The question is also how you are utilizing your resources. A house church without instruments is not likely to employ a brass quintet, but a large church with a fine choir and organ probably should do that for the praise of God at some services. Not all pastors should sing prayers, but in some traditions cantors should teach their pastors how to pray with the elated speech of musical lines. Not all choirs should tackle Bach cantatas, but where the resources and traditions are right the Word should be proclaimed in just this way at some worship services.

The story can take shape in varied ways. The smallest choir and congregation can alternate lines in a hymn to embody the narrative. In "While Shepherds Watched Their Flocks By Night," for example, one person can sing the narration, an individual "angel" can sing the angel's words, and the whole congregation can become the full throng of angels on the last stanza. Aleatory music (literally "chance" music, which allows for spontaneity within a composition), perhaps especially appropriate at Pentecost, can be chosen for choruses of various sizes and abilities. In short, resources must be analyzed and then used fully.

As to gift, the song simply needs to be sung. The people will then be graced with its gift by the God who stands behind it. There is no other way to be, unless the gift is choked off by legalistic restrictions or other self-centered and ingrown destructive impulses. We are often too keen on choking and too slow to accept God's grace, but that grace is in the song whether we know it or not.

This leads to the other half of the question, "Are the people singing?" A more difficult question, but it can be measured with both tangible and intangible measures.

Do the church's acoustics support or destroy singing? Many American churches are designed in such a way that they thwart the very uses for which they are intended. They are covered with carpeting and pew cushions, for example. Sometimes organ and choir are walled off in separated portions of the worship space where they cannot be heard with any clarity or presence. Martin Luther called the church a *Mundhaus*, a mouth-house. Bernard of Clairvaux called the building of churches "geometry in the service of prayer": Cistercian churches were reputedly constructed so that the dropping of a pin would give off the whole overtone series. Joseph Sittler once lamented that a church had carpeted a slate chancel floor; then he remarked that slate is hard like the Word of God.

Churches are places for the Word of God and praise and prayer to resound, to reverberate, to resonate. They ought not be carpeted and draped cotton boxes. The cantor knows this and has to communicate it. This must be communicated in love, but the cantor must ultimately speak a word of judgment on much American church architecture and design because few others know or understand how critical it is to worship. Many people seem to think that churches ought to be extensions of their living rooms. Living rooms are wonderful places, but they are not usually designed for worship. Since seminaries often fail to communicate even the most elementary musical matters, pastors and their people sometimes even think bad acoustics are good. I have been told many times on the telephone by pastors or congregational members that their churches had "excellent acoustics," only to discover dreadful rooms in which sound was immediately soaked up. Singing by choir or congregation is a dismal and demoralizing business in such places. The cantor often turns out to be the only one to champion worship spaces where sound is alive.

Tearing out carpeting and cushions, getting hard surfaces, and doing whatever it takes for sound to resound can be accomplished. And when these things are done, the singing of the people will grow dramatically.[1] Young people who want vital singing will be especially grateful. This is a tangible measure.

Another tangible measure is where people sit and where instruments play. If a few people sit scattered all over a large nave, singing will suffer. If the people sit around the corner from an organ which is in another room off the chancel, singing will suffer. If instruments or choir try to lead the singing from an obscure corner of a dead building, singing will suffer.

Some of these logistics you can control, some you cannot. You may be able to move a choir or instruments if there is space, if you and the pastor and people work it out, and if you do not take up space needed for other things. Moving an organ is less

---

1. For a fuller discussion of this matter see Carl Schalk, "A Lament for Resounding Praise," *The Christian Century*, 100:9 (March 23–30, 1983): 269–271; Scott R. Riedel, *Acoustics in the Worship Space* (St. Louis: Concordia Publishing House, 1986); and Paul Westermeyer, ed., *Meeting House Essays: Acoustics for Liturgy: A Collection of Articles of The Hymn Society in the U. S. and Canada* (Chicago: Liturgy Training Publications, 1991).

likely, but you might be able to tear off dirty grill cloth that stops the sound. Or the church at some point might choose to embark on a renovation program which includes a new organ in a new place and altogether a better worship space. You can champion the people's song in that process. Moving people from accustomed seats may be difficult. People should have the freedom to sit where they please. But if they know why it makes sense to move together to sing, and if ushers are part of the decision-making process and support seating possibilities with you, people might use their freedom to move and to improve the singing.

Good technique—at the organ, with the voice, or with the baton—will encourage good singing. The singing of the choir will improve, and so will the singing of the congregation, even down to technical details of pitch, rhythm, dynamics, and phrasing. If you can execute what you want to do, the song can be sung. If you can't and the song gets sung in spite of you, there is a serious problem. The issue here is not virtuosity; it is technical competence for what you need to do. Private study and practice do wonders. Here progress can be measured, even with behavioral objectives. Our society knows all about technique and how to measure it. Only a little looking will lead you to good teachers, good goals, and measurable improvement.

Good technique is not enough, however. The playing and singing also has to be musical. It is only musicians who fail to get past the printed page and forget music in the process. The rest of humanity does not have that problem. To be human is to sing. Musical leadership will evoke a musical response, and the people's song will be set in motion.

This aspect is more difficult to measure. Behavioral objectives will not help. Your own ear, your own musical instincts, the ears of others, and recording services and listening to them carefully are the kinds of things that are necessary here. If you are honest with yourself, you will know how both your technique and musicianship are faring. Evaluating is actually much easier than accepting God's grace when you miss a note or choose a bad tempo, or mess up a phrase. But that's for the next chapter.

Do you love the people? That may seem like a silly question to ask under the heading, "Are the people singing?" But it is critical. If you hate the people, your playing or singing will show it, and the song will suffer. If you love the people—and that means genuine love, not phony love which is another form of hate—your playing or singing will reflect that love, and the song will blossom. The cantor must be a loving part of the community and must get past just being paid. Only you can measure this one, though plenty of signals from the people will give you their sense of your bearing toward them. If you are at all sensitive, you will get the message.

In addition to measuring the cantor's aspirations by asking whether the Lord's song is being sung, you can look at growth in three other ways. One is to measure it with your peers, which can be done during informal contacts. "Have you read this?" "Did you hear that recording?" "Did you get to the hymn festival?" "What do you think about that idea?" "How do you handle this problem in your church?" Questions like these and the conversations they prompt can be extremely stimulating and can provide the necessary perspective for measuring and invigorating your own work.

Where do these conversations occur? Sometimes they happen on the telephone or in accidental encounters. Mostly they happen at professional meetings of the Hymn Society, the American Guild of Organists, the American Choral Directors Association, the Choristers Guild, denominational church musicians organizations, or workshops sponsored by churches or schools. These meetings are extremely valuable not only for contacts with peers, but for the programs they provide. Programs (sometimes even bad ones) can stimulate all sorts of ideas and can again help you measure your own growth.

Then you can always take actual courses that are offered. It need not be a whole course of study toward a degree. It might be just one or two carefully selected courses at a nearby college, university, or seminary. Courses on church music, hymnody, liturgy and worship, theology and related areas, techniques, musicianship, music theory, music history, and numerous other topics are offered in many places. Some of these are given at summer institutes for a concentrated period of time. Courses offer the most intentional way of analyzing a specific area in which you need help, and of giving you tools and resources for growth in that area.

Another way of looking at growth is to check antagonistic relationships. Sin is really real, not an intellectual construct. The church is partly a human institution, and it participates in all the brokenness that attends our ruptured universe. So, we need to look realistically at the relationships that are less than positive, or even downright negative, and see how growth relates to them.

For example, trying to make changes sometimes generates hostility and negative relationships. My own experience is that, with rare exceptions, church folk are flexible and willing to try many new things. The church is often chastised as being inflexible or unyielding or set in its ways. That rigidness has not been my experience. I have found the secular world far more set in its ways and immovable than the church. The church is usually way ahead on graciousness and flexibility. Nevertheless, hostility can erupt in the church just as it does in the world.

Three ingredients must be present in making healthy changes. First, you have to love the people, genuinely be on their side. Second, what you propose has to make sense. Something totally "off the wall" and foreign to a given tradition is not likely to be supported—and probably should not be. Third, you have to make sure the people understand what you are doing. If those three elements are present, almost anything is possible.

These elements mean, of course, that you cannot simply impose a new notion like a dictator. The people have to be involved in the planning. Remember that you are part of a community. You, like everyone else, have to participate in both its health and its sickness. You may have to compromise since no one person has all the answers, but a compromise can involve healthy growth on your part and need not assault your integrity. There is a difference between a chaotic mishmash and integrity, and people of goodwill can avoid the one and with discussion gradually settle into the other.

You measure your own growth in this process not simply by how many new ideas you have spawned (though, if you have introduced none at all, something is probably wrong), but what kind of community you see emerging. Is it dependent on the promises of God, willing to take risks in the knowledge of God's grace, singing a song of hope into a future of promise, living a life together in which radical disagreement can be expressed because of the bounds of God's love, growing into new life again and again, working for justice and peace in the world? Are you an agent for these things with the people? Are you contributing and leading with your cantorial lyric talents?

In this life, seldom will any unqualified yes be an answer to all these questions. But you can know if the direction is right. You can know if the answers are tilted toward yes rather than no. A little reflection will measure your growth.

In some situations too many of the answers may be no. You may feel out of step with the community. A terrible breach may have developed between you and someone else, more than likely the pastor. In such cases, you have to begin with the assumption that God can be trusted and that the church is indeed the community of forgiveness where new life is possible. We are admonished to go to our brothers and sisters and clear up our quarrels.

When you have done that you may still conclude that things have become unglued in a way you no longer feel is helpful. You may have to say—painfully—that for your growth and that of the people, it is necessary to leave. Such situations do occur. If they occur for you in every parish you serve, you probably need to do some soul-searching. But you need not be devastated by feeling you must leave a given church. Some people's talents fit certain needs at certain times, and other people have talents for other needs at other times. Part of growing is to acknowledge one's own talents and to find when they serve which part of the whole catholic church.

Finally, you have to measure your life as a cantor before God. Growth for the cantor, as for every Christian, does not in the final analysis concern anything we do. It is receiving God's grace again and again. The cantor's role, on the face of it, relates to singing the Lord's song with the people. But behind the face of that song is the face of God searching for the people. To grow is to be discovered by this gracious God. One of the cantor's (and clergy's) major occupational hazards is to be so close to the face and voice of God that we neither see nor hear God ourselves.

So, if it didn't click, turn it back to God. Sing a hymn yourself. Pray, not in the sickly sentiment of phony unctuous "religious" verbiage, but with the cry of the psalmist, "Out of the depths I cry to you, O Lord. Lord, hear my voice." Or, if you received a compliment—and you will receive many—hang loose. You alone know if it went well and whether the compliment was justified. Be gracious. Accept the compliment, but don't let it be your measure. God is the ultimate measure. God's judgment is even harder than yours, and God's grace is greater than yours or any compliment. Accept that grace, and sing a psalm of thanksgiving, "I will give thanks to you, O Lord, with my whole heart." All is of God, and all is for God—even for the cantor.

Chapter 7

Tensions

THE CANTORIAL ROLE IS NOT WITHOUT its tensions. Some of them have already been suggested. Let us first turn to the one alluded to earlier, and at the end of the last chapter, the tension between perfection and grace.[1]

Perfection and Grace

One of the occupational hazards of the artist is the drive for perfection. Musicians, for example, strive to make the sounds of vocal folds, strings, reeds and lips on mouthpieces, sticks on drumheads, and whatever other means is needed, match the ideal they see on the score and hear in their mind. The ideal is virtually never attained. No matter how fine the performance, something could always be better or improved upon. The artistic itch drives the performer to improve, but any performance always remains unsatisfactory either because the ideal becomes more ideal or the details are not improved or because other things go wrong. It's an elusive never-ending spiral.

---

1. For a fuller discussion of this issue, see George B. Caird, "Perfection and Grace," *Duty and Delight: Routley Remembered*, Robin A. Leaver, et al., eds. (Carol Stream: Hope Publishing Company, 1985), 21–33.

When you put art in the service of the church, the demand for perfection is intensified. Not only does the musician have her or his own ideal to contend with; now there is the absolutely unattainable ideal that God demands. It is no accident that the musician who serves a church is often acutely conscious of this ideal and most likely to remind us that God both demands our best and requires we dare not come into the presence of God with anything less than our best.

This ideal can become a heavy burden. The musician strives again and again for the elusive perfection, never achieves it, and always remains both frustrated and guilty over perpetual failure. This is the law. It is the heavy demand, human and especially divine, that relentlessly pounds away until it demoralizes and destroys its victim.

The Christian church knows another reality, grace. God gives it to us, not because we deserve it or merit it or do anything to attain it, but because out of sheer love and goodness God chooses to shower us with blessings and to adopt us as daughters and sons no matter who we are or what we have done. All we have to do is to turn toward God rather than self and accept the gracious gift and promises most fully known in Christ. This is gospel, good news, grace.

The church musician's tension is the tension of any Christian. The tension of perfection and grace is the tension of law and gospel, manifested in a particularly subtle form under the artist's quest for perfection. Two resolutions of this tension resolve nothing and need to be eschewed like the plague.

One is to minimize or forget the gospel and maximize the law. This is not only bad theology; it is also bad living, which will drive one into a corner of a mental institution. The demands of the law cannot be met no matter how hard we try. To try to meet them without the comfort of the gospel is to court disaster. Each seeming success proves to be an illusion, which sets one up for a greater fall. Musicians are particularly adept at putting themselves in this box. To hang one's sanity on achieving the perfect performance—or, for the cantor, the perfect manifestation of the people's song—is ultimately insane. That perfection will never come. You may get close, but even close is ever so far away.

The other resolution to be avoided is to minimize or forget the law and maximize the gospel without regard to the law. Those who choose this option never sound very convincing and only delude themselves when they say, "Well, we know we can't practice very much because we're really busy, so it's okay to make mistakes." Apart from being a lazy cop-out that treats the people with disregard or contempt, it is also bad theology. It is cheap grace—forgiveness without repentance, absolution without confession, grace without discipleship or the cross.[2]

Both perfection and grace, law and gospel must be maximized. The "resolution" here is the paradox of the gospel itself. Christ calls us to be perfect as God is perfect. Not only should we not kill, we are not even to be angry with a sister or brother. Christ raises the legal demand to motives and how one's character is disposed. The demand for perfection that Christ brings is even higher than we can imagine—higher than any musician can imagine. The cantor is called to this demand. The cantor's discipleship is costly—not only in terms of the justice, peace, and neighborly living to which we are all called, but also in terms of musicianship and the highest possible standards of musicianly living as the leader of the Lord's song among the people of God. The demand is not minimized in the least.

On the other hand, the cantor is also forgiven, just like all the rest of us. The cantor's identity, personhood, ego, and self-worth are not dependent on fulfilling musical demands that can never, in the final analysis, be fulfilled. The cantor's selfhood, as for all of us, is dependent on God's grace. Paradoxically, it frees us from the law's demands and frees us to strive to meet those demands with even more energy. We are freed to try and freed to fail, freed to succeed in whatever measure we can, and freed to take risks. The results are not only for living, but for the cantor's

---

2. See Dietrich Bonhoeffer, *The Cost of Discipleship* (New York: The MacMillan Company, 1963), 47 and all of chapter 1, "Costly Grace."

musical doing. The song takes on new life when perfection is not the measure of its integrity or validity, and when the God of love and grace frees us to sing.

Prophet, Priest, and Psalmist

Another tension is suggested by the terms *priestly* and *prophetic*. The priest addresses God on behalf of humanity. The prophet addresses humanity on behalf of God. The language of the priest is prayer. The language of the prophet is a word of judgment and grace. The priest calls the people together where God wills to meet them—in the tent of meeting, to the temple, at the eucharistic table. The prophet speaks a word that smashes the community and reconstitutes it anew.

Music and the musician are often seen primarily in one of these ways. The term *pastoral musician* highlights the priestly. Pastoral activities are priestly activities: prayers and counseling in a confessional setting or at the bedside, meeting God with the sick where God wills to meet us in the Eucharist. The pastoral musician may not do these pastoral priestly activities, but he or she relates to them by emphasizing church music as prayer.

Others see music in prophetic terms. As a contemporary pictorial artist might fracture lines and make a prophetic statement, so the contemporary composer might write dissonant harmonies, angular melodies, and rapidly changing rhythmic patterns. In the church the point of this prophetic music is to afflict the comfortable and to lay bare the anguish of our age along with God's call to address it. The prophetic musician may not preach the Word, but relates to it with prophetic music.

The church musician has both priestly and prophetic roles, to be sure, just like the clergy. Also like the clergy, emphasis on one can compromise the other, though sometimes one or the other is unavoidably required. But the cantor cannot find her or his center in the prophetic or the priestly, because the cantor is fundamentally neither. The cantor is the psalmist, the one responsible for the whole story. As Samuel Terrien pointed out, the psalmists unified

the prophetic and priestly approaches. . . . They offered the pastoral consolations of the priests without
neglecting the moral demands of the prophets. . . .
    Luther rightly called the Psalter "a Bible in minia-
ture." Indeed, the psalms occupy in the Scripture as
well as the church a situation of uniqueness, for they
mirror the faith of Israel as a whole, and they provide a
bridge between moralism, which too easily condemns,
and sacramentalism, which too easily condones. . . .
They kept in tension the equilibrium which must be
maintained between a militant church on earth and a
triumphant kingdom at the end of history.[3]

The cantor is uniquely responsible for singing the whole story
and therefore uniquely responsible for the "equilibrium" that
maintains the proper prophetic-priestly tension. For the cantor to
compromise this equilibrium and move either into the role of
prophet or priest, except under unusual circumstances, is to re-
linquish the uniquely cantorial role.[4]

Political Tensions

Some other tensions are probably not so profound as the first
two, but they may be more annoying. Political tensions are
among these.

The church with its human underside is not devoid of politics. Some church musicians are politicians and jump into the
fray. Some prefer to let the political squabbles rage without their
intentional involvement. All church musicians at some time or
other get pulled into struggles they would just as soon avoid.

Each individual must decide how to deal with these
matters, based both on his or her own personality and on the context. Neither heavy involvement nor lack of involvement is necessarily good or bad. Two points need to be made.

---

3. Samuel Terrien, *The Psalms and Their Meaning for Today* (New York: The
Bobbs-Merrill Company, 1952), 269–270.

4. For a fuller discussion of the issues raised in this discussion, see Francis H.
Williamson, "The Lord's Song and the Ministry of the Church" (Th.D diss., Union
Theological Seminary, 1967), 94–106 and chapters V–VII.

First, if the cantor is doing the job, some political engagement in the life of the parish is inevitable. It does not necessarily mean heavy involvement in everything, which can be detrimental. On the other hand, being totally aloof is hardly possible. Just as good citizenship requires some political involvement, so to be a good member of the body of Christ requires an incarnational involvement in at least some of the politics of the parish—always striving, of course, to maintain one's own integrity in the process.

Second, the cantor is responsible to lobby for the Lord's song, which is the people's song. The people's song requires good acoustics. Lobby for no carpeting. The people's song is genuine and requires what is genuine, not phony. Lobby for real, not canned music, for real instruments, real candles, real flowers, not phony ones. The people and their song deserve careful preparation. Lobby for thoughtful and advanced planning of worship. The people's song is important. Lobby for a budget that reflects its importance. The people's song is for the long haul, not the short run. Lobby for durable and high quality music for several generations of worshipers that young people can grow into rather than out of. In short, keep the needs of the people and their song in mind. You are the people's advocate. If you don't lobby for their song, nobody else is likely to do it. Do it, even when the people themselves do not see what you are doing on their behalf.

Normally you need not be adversarial in these tasks. The church is far more loving, forgiving, and flexible than the secular world. Genuine love does not make good press, so you seldom hear about it. You do hear about the church's squabbles. They do make good press and seem all the more poignant for the church because there the gap between the ideal and the actual is so obvious, and the church is generally pretty honest about itself. You must approach your task with the realization that the church is also prey to the politics of our finite and broken world. Then you must stand fast for the cantorial terrain—the people's song—and struggle for it in the political arena. You do it in love and infinite patience, but with relentless grit, determination, and sometimes the wisdom of the serpent.

The Ideal and the Actual

This tension between the ideal and the actual is both profound and annoying, but it can be one of the most creative. Christ graces the church with his presence until the end of time. The church is an incarnational organism in which the ideal is always incipiently present and waiting to come to expression. The church lives by promise. The kingdom above history and at the end of history is always present in the church. The ideal is always in some sense actual among the body of the baptized.

It is also true that the actual is not always ideal. The church is a human organization in which brokenness and finitude and the rupture Christians call by the code word *sin* are always present. The actual can be pretty dismal sometimes, seemingly far removed from the ideal and the promises of God or the presence of Christ.

For the church musician, this distance from the ideal translates into actual sounds that often leave much to be desired—from the people, choir, organ, or other instruments. At the same time there "steals on" the cantor's "ear the distant triumph song," which somehow is incipiently present in the dismal actual sound. It is cause for hope and despair, and the cantor perpetually lives in that tension.

Trust God's promises. Do not despair. There is hope. Live and work with the people, and you will hear that the "the distant triumph song" also steals on their ears. Do not underestimate old people. They too can sing. Even if they do not agree precisely with what you are doing, if they understand it they are likely to support it and join it. They are among the most flexible members of the society, contrary to popular opinion, because they are free to be flexible. And they are often extremely creative, and able and willing to give their time. Do not underestimate young people. They too can sing. They usually have more seriousness of purpose and think more thoughtfully than their sometimes frenzied facade would suggest. And they can be deeply committed. Do not underestimate anybody. The musically uninformed can be informed, the monotone can learn to sing, the whole body can sing.

Love your people, live with them, sing with them. You will be surprised at how actual the ideal can become.

Personal Tensions

The cantor lives with many personal tensions. The intensity of each one depends on the individual. Here are three of them.

Low Pay

No matter how well you are paid, you will almost certainly not be paid well according to society's standards. If your goal is wealth, the cantor's position is not the one you want. The role has other compensatory benefits, like personal satisfaction and meaningful relationships, but these do not put food on your table and a roof over your head. The tension therefore is not easily resolved even if money is not your goal. Churches and individual church musicians have to work out this issue of compensation as best they can. The solution is not easy. Prepare for the tension.

One Family, Two Churches

Church musicians often feel called to serve churches where their families are not members. That means the family goes to one church on Sunday morning, and the cantor goes to another; the family participates in one set of churchly activities during the week, and the cantor has another. You can sometimes double up or participate in some of the activities of the other, but no completely satisfactory resolution of this tension is possible. You and your family either must learn to live with it by making the necessary accommodations, or the family comes with you, or you quit and go with them. There are no other options.

The Right Position for You

Aspiring to a better position and being content where you are presents yet another tension with no easy solution. It is never easy to tell whether the itch to move is a temptation or a genuine call to more effective service. Each individual must sort out this issue after prayerful reflection. Three general comments can be made, however.

First, it is obviously best if the cantor's abilities and interests match the needs and interests of the parish to be served. Here a mismatch bodes ill for any meaningful service.

Second, to leapfrog from church to church every few months or even every year or two should tell you something is wrong. You do not help the people sing the Lord's song by a sudden splash. You do it piece by piece, brick by brick, with continual dedication and hard work over a long period of time.

Third, there comes a time when your usefulness for a given people in a given place has ended, when you have done what you can do and fresh ideas are needed. Recognize it and leave.

Television Evangelism and the Church

In the contemporary world, one of the tensions the church lives with is generated by television evangelism, sometimes called the "electronic church." By seeming to be church, it sets up a tension about what the church itself is. The church must raise all sorts of questions about this phenomenon, which tells pretty clearly what the church itself is: Where is the cross? Where is discipleship? Where is the body of the baptized? How does the church "take flesh"?

The cantor must ask two other sets of questions. First, what does the "TV church" suggest about worship? How do you worship by remote control? How can you worship without gathering together around word and sacrament?

Second, and most importantly, what does the "TV church" suggest about the people's song? How can the people sing without being together to do it? Is humming along with the television set a viable substitute? Are glitzy, superficial music and commercial, jingle-type texts really what the Lord's song is all about? Can the substance of the story be packaged in such a medium?

The nature of my questions indicates my negative answers to all of them. But I do not mean to be glib about this serious issue. The church needs to take seriously the potentials and possibilities television presents, and we have not done it well. But we also need to say point-blank that much of what happens on the glitzy Christian television shows is precisely what the church is not about, even assuming the purity of the motives of the producers. The church is not about resurrection without death. It is not about life without the cross. It cannot avoid deep societal problems of systemic injustice. It cannot evade tangled problems—like abortion, military buildups, and aid to other governments or rebels—through simplistic answers.

It also needs to be said that television is not a good medium for worship. Worship is not a media event any more than family meals or family celebrations lend themselves to media coverage. Worship requires people to gather together to sing and pray around a book and a table. You don't do that by remote control from your living room couch. Even if you try to televise worship, whatever you put on the screen is only a tiny portion of a multimedia event. That event can only be understood by presence and participation. The cantor knows this distinction and has to communicate it. The people must come to where the song is.

I do not mean television should be eschewed by the church. It should be used creatively, which means you cannot just televise a service. You must edit carefully and selectively so that what you use from a service fits the medium of television. You can't alter worship itself to fit television. Worship has its own dynamics, one of which is gathering together in one place.

Current Issues and Disputes

In every generation the church challenges and is challenged by the culture around it. It causes struggle and dispute. Disputes cause people to take sides. Sometimes these disputes relate directly to the people's song, and sometimes they touch on it more tangentially. In either case, they can cause enough tension that the song virtually comes to a halt. The cantor is caught in the middle of this tension.

Several not unrelated issues exemplify this tension in our period. One is the identity crisis the church faces with virtually every other contemporary institution. Rapid technological change, the pluralism of our period, and impending nuclear disaster (even after the fall of the Berlin Wall) make us uncertain about everything. We walk on constantly shifting sand. We are not sure about values, how to define art, what buildings should look like, what language to use in our worship, whether worship itself has value, or whether there is a norm for anything other than individual feelings. Such a state generates sufficient uncertainty and despair to still the song altogether.

A second issue is inclusive language and hymn-fixing. This broad issue encompasses many smaller ones. Can we use the male pronoun in a generic way? Can we sing about the deaf and the dumb without discriminating against those who cannot hear or speak? Should old hymns which use *he* and *him* be altered so that they no longer project a sexist image? Do terms like *Father, Lord,* and *king* project a male image so that they ought not to be used to refer to God? Do we "desexize" language that refers to humanity, but leave language that refers to God untouched, or do we "desexize" in both categories? How much should we tamper with past texts—updating *thee* and *thy* language is involved here, not only inclusive language—and how much should we leave them alone? In these matters especially, some congregations have experienced a silencing of the song, either because they did not know how to solve the dilemmas or because disagreements were so strong they could not be resolved.

Third, our period is concerned about justice and peace. Symbols of this concern include Martin Luther King Jr., the marches in Selma, the Poor Peoples' Campaign, Archbishop Tutu, ways to combat South African apartheid, women's movements, peace marches, and civil disobedience. The concern can become so intense and the gap between justice and our systemic injustice so great that the song again is silenced.

There are no easy answers to any of these problems, and it is part of our generation's task to struggle with them. I do not mean to suggest how the problems will be solved. That will come with time as the church catholic struggles, sorts out, comes to conclusions, and acts. Several points do need to be made, however.

First, the cantor, pastor, parish, and the whole church *must* struggle together with issues of this sort. Pretending they will go away is a delusion. The frivolous and the superficial will indeed go away, but essential matters of justice, truth, and peace will plague us until they are resolved.

Second, whenever a people perpetuates blatant injustice and tries to sing the Lord's song at the same time, the prophetic cry of Amos is inevitable:

> I hate, I despise your festivals, . . .
> Take away from me the noise of your songs; . . .
> But let justice roll down like waters,
> and righteousness like an ever-flowing stream.
> (Amos 5: 21, 23, 25)

At such times the song needs to come to a halt, for its character has been insidiously violated. Of such occasions, those related to racial justice come readily to mind. But one must be careful here. Pompous and false prophets abound, some of whom cause conflict for their own selfish ends. Every sin of commission or omission is not a cause for the song to stop. The song continues in the midst of human frailty, and the cantor is called to nurture it. The cantor stops it only under the most blatantly unjust conditions.

Third, the song of the church, like its worship, has an almost uncanny capacity to go on as if cultural debates and issues were not occurring at all. This continuation of the song is both positive and negative. On the positive side, it indicates that the church's worship spans the centuries, has more meaning than any single generation can fathom, and challenges the culture itself. On the negative side, it can easily represent the failure of the church to serve or relate to the world around it.

The song of the church, like its worship, also has an uncanny capacity to respond to the culture, which is also both positive and negative. What is positive about it is that it indicates how sensitive the church can be: periods of ferment spawn new hymns, music, and other literature—typified by the current renaissance of hymn writing[5]—which become part of the church's treasured heritage. The negative side is that a too easy response turns the church into a reflection of the world and generates trivial hymns and music.

The cantor lives right in the center of this tension and must keep it strong and healthy. This task requires being sensitive to past forms as well as contemporary currents and refusing to collapse one into the other.

Finally, hymn-fixing, while well-intended, needs careful thought. To alter a word or phrase for purposes of inclusiveness, while at the same time destroying the meter, rhyme scheme, the author's intent or even the meaning of a hymn, obviously creates as many problems as it solves. To tell people to change words as they sing the hymn also engenders considerable confusion, and to write in sloppy changes with scratched-out words gives the impression that hymn-singing is not really important. If hymns are to be altered, alterations must be made with great care. The author's intentions and copyright considerations, along with contemporary needs, are a part of that care. Changing anything in a hymn is a tricky business. It requires time, thought, and skill. Simply scratching out pronouns or anything else that seems offensive is neither just nor successful.

On the other hand, hymn-fixing is not really about changing a few words like *he* or *him* or *she* or *her*. The heart of the matter is idolatry and justice. God is not made in our image, male or female. All anthropomorphisms are at best broken symbols, and in Christ there is neither Jew nor Greek, male nor female, slave nor free. All of humanity—black, white, Spanish-speaking, female, male, handicapped, heterosexual, homosexual, rich, poor, third world, sick, healthy—is loved by God. We are to treat one another justly and equally as brothers and sisters. What we sing is therefore of great consequence, because it both indicates and shapes what we believe and how we act. Either to change a few

5. See Paul Westermeyer, *With Tongues of Fire: Profiles in 20th-Century Hymn Writing* (St. Louis: Concordia Publishing House, 1995)

pronouns without thought or to avoid the problem altogether is to treat a serious matter blithely. The whole church needs to discuss these matters thoughtfully and carefully, and cantors need to contribute their insights to the discussions.

The Real Tension

Theologically the tension headed "The Ideal and the Actual" could have been expressed with the terms realized and unrealized eschatology. In Christ the eschaton—the end of time, the consummation, the fulfillment—has broken in among us. It is therefore in some sense realized.

In Christ we know it. Yet it is known by faith, not by sight. While the victory has been won by Christ, all the skirmishes are not over, and we still live between the times of Christ's first and final coming. All the troubles of what is as yet unrealized still attend us.

The tension of *realized* and *unrealized* eschatology is the key to all the tensions in this chapter, not just the one titled "The Ideal and the Actual." Because we live between the times, we can expect all the tensions I have alluded too—and more. That we can sing together at all is a mystery, a gift, and a sign of the realized presence of Christ among us.

Chapter 8

Clergy-Musician Relationships

IN THE LAST PARAGRAPH OF *Church Music and Theology*, Erik Routley wrote,

> It will remain bad theology so long as the theologian and the artist refuse to communicate with one another; as long as the theologian regards the artist as fundamentally a temperamental trifler, and the artist the theologian as an obstinate and ignorant theorist, the best we shall get is patronage from church to music, together with tentative moralisms from musicians to musicians. At worst it will be, as it often in practice is, a wicked waste of an opportunity for glorifying God through fruitful partnership.[1]

Though Routley subsequently updated his book with another,[2] these words have not lost their power. And, if you substitute *pastor* or *priest* or *minister* (or your favorite term) for *theologian*, and *cantor* or *church musician* (or your favorite term) for *artist*, Routley's words are still relevant.

---

1. Erik Routley, *Church Music and Theology* (Philadelphia: Muhlenberg Press, 1959), 110.
2. Erik Routley, *Church Music and the Christian Faith* (Carol Stream: Agape, 1978).

Pastor and cantor can form a most powerful partnership. It implies what Routley expresses: when the partnership is not grasped and utilized, the result is "a wicked waste of an opportunity for glorifying God" and serving humanity.

Examples of Nonpartnerships

There are many examples of nonpartnerships that sometimes masquerade as partnerships. So let us first clear the deck of all the nonpartnerships—the wicked wastes.

The Pastor as Manipulator

This pastor skillfully shapes everything in the congregation's life by manipulating people and situations. Everything must go as the pastor plots it, and only the pastor is privy to the plot. The pastor gives the appearance of welcoming constructive engagement by people and committees in the parish, but in fact all dialogues and suggestions are skillfully orchestrated or silenced by the pastor.

In this case the pastor spends much time putting out fires of dissent, dropping hints at proper moments, working behind the scenes to pack councils and committees with those who will not rock the boat or raise difficult questions. On the surface a congregation with this type of pastor can appear extremely successful because everything seems to be going in one direction with an apparent sense of purpose. Under the surface dissent can seethe for long periods.

Worship must also fit the mold of the pastor. The demands of the liturgy and the rights of the people in assembly are skillfully diminished to match the pastor's private plot. The pastor does not preside. He or she controls all the planning and the doing of worship by skillful under-the-surface movement.

Music, of course, must also fit the pastor's scheme. Its dynamics as handmaiden of the liturgy are denied. And the church musician who wishes to remain employed in this environment can never contribute her or his skills or insights into planning or even playing the service. The musician in this situation learns quickly by subtle, but not too subtle, signals about what the pastor expects. And the musician simply carries that out or looks for another job.

This is not a partnership. It is a wicked waste.

The Pastor as Dictator

The pastor who is dictator does not worry about under-the-table control. This pastor simply controls everything right out front, and that's that. People and staff all follow the bidding of the king or queen, no questions asked.

This pastor usually has a plan, makes it known, follows it, and expects those in the community to follow it also. Those who don't like it can leave. A perfectionist with some charisma can often make this scenario work because the sense of purpose and vision along with proper adroit political control can generate a considerable following.

But worship and music are again denied their dynamics. They are part of the package of the pastor as solo performer. The musician's gifts are to be used as the dictator dictates. Advice and suggestions are to be given by the cantor only when they are sought. Otherwise the cantor understands quite clearly that he or she is simply to do the pastor's bidding. Again, this is a wicked waste of a possible partnership.

Chaos-Control

There are some pastors who control everything, but they do it by chaos. These pastors reserve decision making to themselves, but refuse to make decisions until the last minute.

A good example is the pastor who will not choose hymns until Saturday afternoon or evening or perhaps even Sunday morning. I have been told of one such instance where the secretary of the church came in to type or run off bulletins at those eleventh hour times. The organist, of course, usually got the hymns just before the service.

In this case, and similar ones, the organist has no time for planning or practice. Yes, of course, many organists could sight read any hymn chosen. But is there no more creativity to hymn-playing than sight-reading? And what about linking other service music to the hymns? All this is denied the organist—and the choir director—by the pastor who exercises chaos-control. This nonpartnership is again a wicked waste.

The Pastor Assumes the Musician Is a Trifler

Ministers with this assumption may take quite different stances on how they relate to their people. They may control as manipulator or dictator, they may exercise chaos-control, they may be pastoral, they may welcome dialogue, or they may have no model. But on one thing they are agreed: the musician is a trifler and probably a temperamental one.

This minister assumes that what the musician does is not very important. The minister knows somehow that the musician has to be there (and may be offended by that knowledge), but what the musician does is not considered valuable. That tempo, pacing, celebration, mourning, surprise, and the church's song itself might be related to the cantor's responsibility has never crossed this pastor's mind. This pastor may even choose to control tempos by loud singing. The musician is viewed as an appendage who is tolerated.

Usually, however, this pastor sees the musician not only as a trifler. In this mind-set, the musician is almost invariably viewed as temperamental. That viewing someone as a trifler might set off his or her temper is apparently not considered by this pastor, but, in fairness to the pastor, musicians often are artistic types who may be temperamental. Musicians also can be as rational, caring, and helpful as any other group of people, however, given the chance. Viewing them as temperamental triflers is yet another wicked waste.

The Pastor Assumes the Cantor Is a Hired Hand

This position is a variation of the last one. The minister here may recognize the importance of the cantor and may seek out a fine one, but the cantor is viewed as someone you buy—like a race horse. The cantor must have technical prowess and maybe even musical sensitivity. You buy those things as you buy a commodity in the grocery store. You don't consider that the cantor has any deeper responsibilities as a servant of the church or as a pastoral musician.

This perspective, perhaps inadvertently, is fostered now by many pastors, musicians, and churches who demand elaborate contracts. Contracts are valuable. They guard against chaos and misunderstanding, and they spell out obligations to protect both sides to the agreement. But when elaborate detail is demanded down to so many minutes a week, the inevitable result is to regard the cantor as a hired hand. Cantors and pastors who have experienced grace in the body of Christ know another reality and life together. This perspective does not foster it and turns out to be one more wicked waste.

The pastor so far has caused the wicked wastes at partnership, but musicians can be equally guilty. So let us work through some of the musician's unpartnerlike perspectives in a kind of free crab canon. We can be briefer here because the dimensions of the various perspectives have already been sketched.

The Musician Assumes a Business Relationship

The musician who assumes working in a church is totally reducible to a business relationship of hours and pay precludes partnership. This person may be competent. Competence should be rewarded. It is legitimate to expect to be paid and to know how much. The laborer is worthy of her or his hire.

But to take the legalistic details as the substance of the relationship is a temptation to which the musician is probably more prone than the pastor. The partnership is at best superficial and usually nonexistent in such a case. There is another possibility and another life together. This perspective is one of the wicked wastes which stops that possibility before it can even start.

The Musician Assumes the Pastor Is a Theorist

Some church musicians assume their craft is practical and the pastor's is theoretical. They also assume that practice is better than theory, which means they conclude the pastor is an impractical fool of some sort.

This position is usually accompanied by Routley's adjectives, "obstinate and ignorant." The pastor is considered not just a theorist, but an obstinate and ignorant one. Such an assumption is obviously not calculated to achieve goodwill. That it might make a potentially flexible pastor become obstinate does not cross the musician's mind, and the result is one more wicked waste.

The Technician

Musicians obviously have to develop their technical skills. That necessity leads some church musicians to assume technique is an end in itself. That assumption leads to another: that the job of the church musician is reducible to technique. For the organist, it's finger and pedal technique. For the choral conductor, it's choral technique. For the singer, it's vocal technique.

Apart from the purely musical problem with this perspective—namely, that music is reducible solely to technical considerations—it simply fails to consider deeper responsibilities or anything beyond the surface of technical competence. It surely does not allow for a partnership with the pastor because it so narrowly restricts the role of the musician. It leads once more to a wicked waste.

The Cantor as Dictator

For the cantor to be the dictator requires the right circumstances, because the church musician is not usually positioned to wield such power. But long tenure, influential friends with money, or a strong personality (which some musicians possess abundantly) can make the cantor aggressively and relentlessly dictatorial.

What often happens here is that the worship and other life of the church revolve around the concert pretensions of the musician. Pastor and people wind up subservient to the performer.

Even if the musician does have some sensitivity to worship, if she or he manages to control everything without others' ideas and creativity, the result is still a solo performance. It precludes partnership and turns into one more wicked waste.

The Cantor as Manipulator

The manipulative cantor is much more common than the dictatorial one because, as I indicated, the musician is not usually positioned to dictate. He or she can easily manipulate, however, especially if the proper personality traits are present.

This person knows how to seek out the right people, to play up to wealthy families, to pull political strings, to choose music which will sell to the right people, and to force the pastor into decisions in the interests of the cantor. The control is always covert, never overt, but it is exerted tenaciously and intensely. And it is one more wicked waste.

The cantor who manages to become either dictator or manipulator probably perpetrates on the congregation a more demonic evil than the pastor who dictates or manipulates. The pastor must control with some breadth and perspective. The demands of various components of parish life like worship, preaching, social issues, evangelism, counseling, and teaching include built-in checks and balances. The church musician who controls usually operates from the limited perspective of one aspect of Christ's body, the musical one. The musician is less likely to attain control, therefore, but once attained, the control can be far more demonic and can skew the life of a congregation far more dangerously.

No Dialogue

In some situations, neither pastor nor cantor is solely at fault. The two simply do not communicate. Each does what she or he thinks is required by the respective job description (implicit or explicit), and neither goes further than that. There is no malice necessarily between the two. They simply have not considered that any partnership is possible or beneficial.

No Dialogue With Malice

This situation represents a conscious decision not to communicate. Pastor and musician may have opposite points of view and refuse to discuss or share them with the other. They may have a personality conflict they refuse to resolve. They may mutually regard one another as temperamental trifler and obstinate theorist. Whatever the reason, they simply refuse to communicate. Each goes his or her own way with no partnership, and worship for the people becomes aggressively schizophrenic.

Roles of Clergy and Cantor

An analysis of the things clergy and cantor do helps to clarify why the potential for nonpartnership is so easily present. A number of responsibilities can be isolated for both persons. Let us begin with the pastor.

The Pastor's Study

A library study of some sort invariably accompanies the pastor. Library study space points to the studying the pastor continually needs to do. The pastor's tools are books, journals, and words. These words cover at least biblical, theological, historical, pastoral, ethical, and liturgical subjects.

All of us know pastors who do not study—sometimes because pastoral and administrative responsibilities eat up their time and strength, or they choose to do these at the expense of study. Sometimes it's because they are lazy. But even those pastors have to do some reading, and the ideal and necessity for study always loom over them. They are inescapable. The responsible pastor finds a way to study, for when he or she neglects it, the parish is the poorer.

Sermon Preparation

One of the critical tasks of the pastor is sermon preparation. Much study is geared toward this responsibility, but it also requires a sensitive alertness to the contemporary world and congregational needs. It cannot be done apart from involvement with the people, but at the same time it requires hours of preparation alone in a study.

Sermons often have a bad name because so many boring travelogues, moralisms, ethical admonitions, and other pompous nonsense get passed off as sermons. A sermon is far more important than any of that and lays on the pastor a heavy duty and a joyous delight. The pastor must struggle with the biblical text and biblical message along with the contemporary situation so that by God's grace, her or his words are heard as the Word of God itself. That Word, in all its permutations, is at heart an announcement of grace and love.

The paradox is that all the struggle and study in the world will not produce the word of grace, yet the word of grace will not be spoken without the pastor's struggle and study. The genuine pastor takes this task seriously and devotes much time to it.

The prophetic word sometimes drives the pastor to social and ethical activities in the world: picketing nuclear power plants, putting bodily self on the line against racial injustice, struggling on behalf of the poor and oppressed, challenging systemic injustice, and being Christ to the neighbor where the need demands it. In recent years, while many false pompous prophets have appeared, we have also witnessed the courageous activity of Martin Luther King, Jr., and others less well-known but equally genuine. The call to this activity is inescapable at times and sets up for the pastor a potentially devastating tension between the pastoral and prophetic responsibilities.

Worship Leader

The pastor is ordained to preach the Word and celebrate the Sacraments. Leadership in worship grows out of both these responsibilities, but especially the sacramental one. Just as the host at a banquet prepares carefully and thoughtfully for his or her guests, so the pastor on behalf of the host who is Christ prepares carefully and thoughtfully for those who come weekly to the eucharistic banquet. (In those churches where the Eucharist is not celebrated weekly, that ideal still hangs over their celebrations and in large measure controls them.)

Presiding at worship means planning prayers carefully, training acolytes and readers, practicing reading, preparing for the flow of the service, planning when to get out of the way, knowing and studying the Propers for the service, knowing how one service relates to another and to the whole church year, and generally planning how to preside graciously and as helpfully as possible for the guests at Christ's table.

Pastoral Care

A responsible pastor serves the needs of the parish with pastoral care in many different situations. The pastor rejoices with parents who have a baby, weeps with those who suffer illness and death, visits the sick, counsels those with marital dilemmas, listens to parents' problems with children and children's problems with parents, celebrates weddings and other occasions for merrymaking, and walks alongside the congregation in all their joys and sorrows. Sometimes situations are convoluted and require a high energy level for long periods of time. Sometimes they are simple and more relaxed. In all cases and at all times the responsible pastor is alert and responsive to the needs of the people she or he serves.

Teaching

A good pastor is usually a good teacher. She or he teaches in contexts not formally labeled classes and also in classes themselves, including Sunday School classes, new-member classes, confirmation classes, and any number of special courses or lectures in and out of the local church. The topics a pastor may have to cover include ones of his or her expertise, but they generally include ones in which knowledge is more limited. Both types require preparation, study, research, and care.

Administration

Studies indicate pastors spend much of their time on administrative tasks. Administration includes managing, organizing, acting as executive secretary, and generally keeping the institution of the parish running smoothly.

A pastor is called to be a servant of the servants of God. A willingness to do the menial tasks is commendable. But administration can eat up all the time in the week, especially in our society of bureaucracies, forms, numbers, junk mail, and paper blizzards that continuously litter desks. Pastors must do administrative tasks, but they are always dangerous because they eat away at pastoral counseling, sermon preparation, worship planning, teaching, and study.

The Cantor's Practice

If study inevitably accompanies the pastor, practice inevitably accompanies the church musician. Technique and technical facility are required if the organist is to play, the singer is to sing, or the conductor is to conduct. Exercises of one sort or another as well as the practice of actual music are part and parcel of the cantor's normal activity.

We all know church musicians who do not practice, either because they are lazy or because demands on their time and energy (like the necessity to earn a living in some field other than music) eat up their practice time. We put up with the result, namely, that the music is performed poorly. Even the cantor who is extremely facile needs to practice. Practice is an inevitable concomitant of the cantor's trade.

Practice involves score study. The serious musician is forced to study the score to find out what its inner logic is, to discover how it should be performed, and to read and learn all about its composer and context to help in its realization. This is real study, and at first glance it looks like the study of the pastor. It is not quite the same, however. It is always geared to practice and performance in a way that the pastor's study is not. For the cantor it is derivative, and the cantor can avoid the study in a way the pastor cannot. The cantor avoids it at her or his own peril, of course, but the result of that avoidance will never be quite so obvious for the cantor as it is for the pastor. It is equally as detrimental, but it can be more easily hidden.

Apart from actual score study, the serious cantor will read books and journals about church music and the tasks of the church musician. These sources are not nearly so numerous nor do their topics range so widely as the pastor's. Except in the case of musicology or complex tabulations in areas like music education, they are written in a somewhat breezier style than biblical or theological studies. Again, the cantor avoids this study at his or her own peril, but with somewhat fewer deleterious effects than the pastor.

Rehearsal Leader

Practice is for performance, and the church musician as church musician performs in two contexts: rehearsals and services. For every well-prepared service, hours of rehearsing have been spent in preparation. I do not have in mind here individual practice. I mean rehearsing with others, to which the cantor's own practice is partly given over. It includes rehearsing with choirs, soloists, instrumentalists, the pastor if she or he sings, and perhaps even the congregation. Both amateurs and professionals are involved, and the conductor or accompanist prepares for them in different ways. In the case of amateurs, more teaching will obviously be present.

The Cantor as Worship Leader

The other performance context for the church musician is the worship service itself. The individual practicing and group rehearsing is geared to this occasion. Here the finest artistry is required—not for itself, of course, but as a means to the glory of God. Music is modified in the context of worship. It is no longer a performance as the world views concerts or recitals. It is another sort of performance—a part of worship. That distinction alters and heightens its importance, ideally requiring even more preparation and care than the concert world gives music.

The cantor, especially the one who is also the organist, leads worship through music. In large measure she or he controls a service's flow, pacing, and tone. "Performing" for a service, therefore, is not only performing a piece or pieces in isolation. It is molding them into a whole service which, like music, spins itself out through time. The music of worship needs careful planning and preparation week by week and service by service.

Cantors also give concerts and recitals. While necessary for their lives as musicians, concerts and recitals are ancillary to their role as cantors. Cantors use their experience from recitals and concerts, however, in their service playing, singing, and conducting.

Teacher

A cantor is invariably a teacher. Organists and vocalists have private organ and voice students; conductors teach music to choirs, soloists, and instrumentalists; organists, choir directors, and soloists usually have to teach congregations at some point; and formal classes about topics related to church music—like hymnody, music history, organ design, the role of music in the church—invariably require teaching by the cantor.

Here a kind of study and preparation similar to that of the music educator is required. It is likely to be somewhat less lecture-oriented than the pastor's teaching, because music—especially sung music—uniquely involves sound and participation. I make this statement with full knowledge that many pastors teach by means of discussion groups or an inductive method, which involves doing by their students. By its very nature, however, music demands doing in a way that a class on theology or ethics or church history does not. It means the musician prepares to teach not only by study, but by practice as well.

Administration

Depending on the size of the church's program, the cantor may have more or fewer administrative duties. This cannot be avoided. Unlike the pastor's administering, the musician's is not over the whole church. But music has to be chosen, organized, catalogued; people have to be called; programs have to be planned; rehearsals have to be scheduled and organized; the paper blizzard has to be attended to; and the machinery has to be kept oiled. As for the pastor, the cantor needs to do all these things, but with care, so they do not eat up all the time. Our society has a way of turning everything into administration, as if it were an end in itself. It is not. The cantor is the musical servant of the servants of God and has important things like music to attend to.

Perspective

When you stand back and view the roles of clergy and musician, you get a picture like this: The pastor studies and meets the people through the prophetic, sacramental, and pastoral word. The cantor practices and meets the people through the sung word. Both teach, though the kind of teaching differs. Both have administrative responsibilities, again somewhat different in kind.

The potentials for conflict are clear. The clergy is trained to think. The cantor is trained to perform. The clergy, unless she or he has attended one of a few rare seminaries, probably has had little or no musical training and, strange as it may seem, probably not much training in worship either—all of which can lead to a vague though palpable defensiveness. The musician has probably had little or no theological training. Because he or she has more ecumenical opportunities than does the pastor, the musician may have a better feel for worship through experience and instinct, but that feel is usually inchoate and therefore not sufficiently formulated to be communicated in an articulate way to the pastor or anybody else.

Since the pastor and cantor are trained differently and do different things, they often view things differently. The pastor may see all of worship related to preaching, pastoral care, social action, ethics, or, most recently, evangelism. The musician may see all of worship related to art as the world views art, or to teaching higher standards of taste, or to a perfect performance. These widely divergent perspectives obviously offer the potential for substantial conflict, especially when planning and communication are lacking. If the clergy and cantor hold different perspectives and then never meet one another and do no planning together, the schizoid condition of much American worship is the inevitable result.

Solution

It need not be so. The way out of the dilemma begins with worship, not with the leaders of worship.

Worship is the *work of the people*. That's what *liturgy* means. Worship in assembly is corporate. It is not the work of one person. It is the work of the people together. It has a rhythm in which individuals fade in and out of view for the sake of the whole body.

Worship does not happen without leaders. Any corporate gathering requires leaders, and worship has many of them—from readers to greeters to ushers to singers, to altar guild and acolytes. Two leaders are critical: the pastor and the cantor. If they lead well and work together, a powerful partnership for the people results. If they do not work together, we have a wicked waste.

Minister and cantor need to begin with the fundamental presupposition that they are in this together *for the people*. Once that assumption is made, the rest is comparatively easy. If that assumption is not made, the rest is hopeless.

The minister presides. Because the minister presides and "by virtue of his or her training, knowledge, pastoral responsibility, and personal presence," he or she "contributes the most to the overall unity, style, and flow of the liturgy."[3] A pastor who presides well is not a one-person show, however. A good presiding minister knows how to get out of the way when assistants and readers take their parts.

Mostly the good presiding minister gets out of the way when the cantor assumes a leadership role. A sensitive cantor— usually an organist in our culture—responds to the flow the pastor sets and then controls the pacing and tone of a service by the

---

3. Frank C. Senn, *Christian Worship and Its Cultural Setting* (Philadelphia: Fortress Press, 1983), 126.

tempo of hymns and service music, by the nature of introductions, by spacing after silence or lessons, by the choice of harmonizations, by dynamics, and by the choice of and approach to all the other music in the service.

Throughout the service, both pastor and cantor assume leadership roles in tandem. When they work together, a remarkable partnership exists. When they work at cross purposes or no purposes, the result is a wicked waste.

How does the partnership come about? There is no single recipe for every pastor and cantor. (In the next chapter I will suggest one that worked best for a pastor and me in the last church I served.) In some cases the pastor may choose hymns; in others the musician may do it. For some partnerships, few meetings together may be required; for others, many meetings. Part of the actual working together depends on the age, training, background, and experience of the partners. An experienced pastor and a high school organist will have a different working relationship from an experienced organist and a pastor just out of seminary. Whatever the working relationship, the two need to communicate so that each understands what the other is doing and why. And each needs to be free to question and challenge the other in a dialogue of grace. Such a dialogue leads to a powerful partnership, which helps us all worship God in spirit and truth.

The People

Clergy-cantor relationships pose a serious problem for the contemporary church. Meetings of church musicians or meetings of clergy reveal what a prime topic it is. Since this book, broadly speaking, is about leaders in the church, and since the relationship of two of those leaders does pose such a serious challenge today, I have addressed it in some detail.

But we must not lose sight of a third party to this partnership, namely, the people. Clergy and cantor may work together very well for the people, only to find that someone or some group in the congregation undermines and destroys their efforts. A local church does not consist only of clergy and cantor working separately or even together. It is a team effort in which the people are also called to play their part faithfully.

The people can be as unfaithful as the cantor or clergy. This unfaithfulness often expresses itself in attempts at dictatorial or manipulative control. The tenor who sits in the same choir pew every Sunday for twenty-three years and refuses to move is attempting to control selfishly. So is the man who brags about paying all the church's bills or the woman who gives enough money to start a new congregation because "the organist plays too loud." I have heard of mothers who bribed organists with large sums of money so they would play certain pieces of music at their daughters' weddings. There are those who try to work cantor against pastor, pastor against cantor, or other staff members against one another for selfish ends. They can refuse to help make decisions, yet boycott meetings where decisions are made or mount rumor campaigns after the meetings. They can covertly and overtly harass in order to control music or preaching or anything else they want to control.

In all these examples, the individuals who attempt to control are concerned with themselves and not with the good of the whole congregation. Like cantor and pastor, the people also have to see that they are part of a community whose story transcends theirs, and that the good of others is equally as important as their own good.

Some members may not attempt to control at all. They may mean well by suggesting what seems positive: a careful contract or rules for the use of the building or a room, for example. These people, often businesspeople, are valuable resources, as long as they do not lose sight of the community of grace. If legalistic restrictions are seen as the substance of a congregation's being, something is wrong. These people need to learn another reality in which rules and regulations are seen in the light of the transcending love and forgiveness of God. Otherwise the song itself, along with the life together, will be stifled.

Postscript

In many congregations, pastor, people, and cantor get along well, work together, sing the Lord's song, and live together as the community of grace they are called to be. We do not hear about them because they go about their business quietly, without glitz, and because their life together gives the media nothing to report. The media thrives on conflict, and when conflict is handled by a community of grace the media searches for news elsewhere.

These churches are by no means perfect. But they know the gift of song, which expresses the presence of Christ among them. That song always steals on the ear and calls for any relational problems of pastor, clergy, and people to be resolved. The resolution ultimately resides in an ear that hears beyond the self for the good of the whole. That ear, like the song itself, is a gift of God's grace all congregations can receive for the taking.

Chapter 9

Heart to Heart

WHEN I SENSED THE NEED FOR A BOOK of this sort, I asked several people about the idea, among them my doctoral advisor Martin E. Marty. As he had done for my dissertation, he graciously helped me to order my ideas and say what I wanted to say. He suggested that the concluding chapter (in this second edition, it is the third chapter from the end) be a "semi-autobiographical confession from one cantor to another." "Talk about your vocation," he said. "Do a case study."

I had not planned that. Academically I have been trained to assemble all the data I can, analyze and synthesize it, then write as objectively as possible and usually with copious footnotes. Autobiography, even prefixed with "semi," is probably less than objective and certainly not terribly easy for me to write. But, when I reflected on Dr. Marty's suggestion, I had to conclude that he was probably right on target.

Whenever I have given lectures or workshops, I have always tried to organize material coherently so that details fall into place in some sort of synthesis. Often I have discovered, however, that the true synthesis comes in the question-and-answer period when someone says, "What do you do when . . . ?" Then I have to become "semi-autobiographical," explain my situation, and indicate what I might do. Then also the bones of details I have presented take on flesh and begin to make sense from my perspective as a specific church musician in a specific church, which in turn allows people to apply or adapt those details more easily to their own situations. So here's a heart-to-heart, "semi-autobiographical," question-and-answer case study. I wish I could also have the give-and-take of your "case studies" as I do at workshops, because I usually learn from them. But I hope the give here without the take will pull things together and be of value for you.

When I wrote the first edition of this book, I was cantor at Ascension Lutheran Church in Riverside, Illinois, a moderate-sized parish in the Chicago metropolitan area. I directed the choir, played the organ, and was responsible for all the music related to worship. The position was part-time. We had one service each Sunday. One choir rehearsed each Wednesday night and sang each Sunday from about September to May. The choir had fourteen members or so, distributed equally among the parts (two to four to each part). Some of them had musical training, some did not. They were volunteers from the congregation and were not paid. I did have a budget to pay instrumentalists or soloists, as needed, however, and I used it.

The congregation was a mix of young and old with no unusual musical talent. They were a delightful group of people to work with, just like the choir itself and every other congregation I have served. They did not all agree about everything, but they shared their disagreements. They had no more training in worship and music than most congregations and represented a pretty normal cross-section of backgrounds, abilities, careers, and economic status.

When I was chosen as cantor, the congregation wanted someone who would work with the pastor in planning worship and music, who would be concerned about the song of the people, and who would focus on music related to worship. They suggested calling me *cantor* before I mentioned it, a pleasant indication of common ground. They did not require a flashy virtuoso, but were looking for someone who was competent, who understood the nature of church music, who would spend time planning carefully, and who would help them solve the problems they had with their organ.

I felt called to take this position in part because my abilities and interests seemed to match the church's needs and interests. I have only moderate musical abilities, but I have developed them to some degree of competence as a choir director and service organist. (This order is in no sense normative. It simply is what happened in my life. However one's abilities and training have developed, they can be further developed for the cantorial role if a person is willing to make the necessary adjustments and do the proper study and practice.) I had served as choir director or choirmaster/organist for worshiping communities since I was a freshman in high school, in small, moderate, and large churches, part-time and full-time. A goodly portion of my formal and informal study had been generated by questions those experiences raised: from the undergraduate music major to seminary, to school of church music, to the doctorate in church history in which theology, worship, and music were the substance of my research. I had thought quite a bit about the issues this parish was raising and had had experience solving them. I felt I could be of service to the parish and could meet its needs.

It was not easy to take this position because it meant leaving the church nearer my home where my family and I were members, a church I had been serving as choir director. We had to struggle as a family with that change. It was always painful for me to pull out of my driveway alone every Sunday morning and drive several communities away—even though my family was attending a service nearer home with the same lessons and in many other ways largely the same as the one where I was cantor. The same or not, we were not together around one pulpit and one table, and that was painful indeed. It's one of the cantorial tensions I experienced quite personally.

For my full-time work I was teaching at Elmhurst College, a school in the Chicago area of which the brother theologians Reinhold and H. Richard Niebuhr were graduates. I directed the choirs there; taught courses related to church music, hymnody, and worship; and chaired the Music Department. I enjoyed the teaching immensely, and I had some wonderful relationships with students, choir members, colleagues, secretaries, administrators, and staff members. In many respects, however, my full-time job was similar to the jobs of most people in the late twentieth century, whether we work in factories or offices or wherever: I too had to struggle with a faceless, mindless, rootless, and visionless bureaucracy.

But when I went to work as a cantor at church, I entered a sea of sanity in a world of insanity. The church where I worked was by no means perfect. It had its share of disagreements, disappointments, frustrations, struggles, and unhappy times. But the pastor grappled with the Word of God and with us. We gathered weekly around Word and Sacrament. Where the world sought security and therefore death, the church was willing to take risks, because it lived by promise and life. It did not have to succeed. It was free to fail and to succeed. Where the world lives by legalistic fictions, the church lives by grace. We could disagree—even violently—and still love each other because the love of a gracious God stands above and embraces our disagreement. Into this world of sanity at this church, and most of the others I have served, I was privileged to make music and to sing the Lord's song with this people of God.

I put in well over a forty-hour workweek at my college job (often more than double that), but I still found fifteen to twenty hours for my cantorial one. Sometimes the number was less, sometimes more, depending on the time of the year. The forty-hour workweek is a safeguard against injustice by unscrupulous employers, but it is a fiction for one's own schedule. Each day has sixteen to eighteen waking hours. Even with the equivalent of one or two days taken out of the week for recreation and time with the family, eighty to one hundred eight hours still remain. Part-time cantorial posts are quite possible.

My week as cantor looked something like this: Usually on a Tuesday or Thursday evening I would attend a meeting with a committee. It was sometimes held briefly on Sunday after church, and some weeks had two meetings or no meetings at all. Once a week, usually some morning, the pastor and I met for one to several hours. Wednesday evening was always reserved for choir rehearsals. Part of Saturday, usually the morning, was saved for organ practice, unless my family had an activity or I was leading a workshop, in which case I had to move this practice to another time.

During the week I worked several things into my schedule whenever and wherever I could fit them in: score study; daily practice if at all possible, however brief, at a piano when I couldn't get to an organ; writing (hymn texts, articles for the church paper, letters, notes for classes); composing and arranging music and copying parts; planning ahead; making final plans for the immediate Sunday and getting that information in to the church office for the bulletin; and phone calls to church, parishioners, choir members, instrumentalists, publishers (usually for copyright permissions), or anyone else who had to be called.

On Sunday I usually arrived at the church by 8:30 A.M. or so to warm up and make a final check for registrations at the organ, the choir rehearsed at 9:30, and the service began at 10:00. After the service I spent some time seeing people I needed to see or to greet others. Sometimes I returned later in the day for another service.

During the summer this schedule changed because there were no choir rehearsals, fewer meetings, and an earlier service time. The pastor and I still met except when vacations intervened. I tried to spend some complete summer days or even weeks planning ahead and ordering music for the coming year. Though I knew my plans would probably change, at least I had an overall scheme for the year. If the pastor and I had planned that far ahead (the longer I was there, the farther ahead we planned), I could work my choosing into those plans; if not, my choosing was more provisional.

At Christmas and Holy Week the schedule also changed. Extra rehearsals and services required that I was likely to be at church much more often practicing for a whole set of back-to-back services. Holy Week especially required clearing time almost exclusively for cantorial responsibilities. This task was more or less complicated depending on the timing of spring break in the college calendar.

The content of my schedule was more important than its external details. It was satisfying partially because of the work with the people and partially because of the work with the pastor. The first of those components has almost always been present in any church situation I have worked in, the second not so often. In this sense I was unusually fortunate. Though our styles were different, Pastor Paul Landahl and I came to value our work together and put behind us a situation where pastor and cantor pass like ships in the night (or proceed on a collision course).

We hit on a scheme that worked for us. It is surely not the only possibility, but I share it for others to consider. When we met weekly, we discussed all sorts of matters related to our work in the parish, but mostly we planned worship services. Our goal was always to be at least several months to a year ahead in our planning so that music could be chosen, bought, and rehearsed in advance, and all other arrangements for services completed in time.

For each service we worked through the lessons and other propers together. Sometimes it involved getting out commentaries and doing some exegesis. Sometimes it was simpler. In all cases it meant getting a feel for the particular service and understanding its themes. We surrounded ourselves with Bibles, commentaries, hymnals, hymnal companions, and worship planning aids, then chose hymns, decided how we would use them, made tentative decisions about all the aspects of a given service, and the pastor came to some conclusions about the sermon topic.

We then went our separate ways to work out what we had begun. I worked on hymns and chose organ and choral music based on our planning, then got it prepared. The pastor fleshed out the sermon and worked at the prayers. We sometimes had to discuss the service again or change our minds later, but we were both on board together from the beginning and knew what the other was doing.

On some occasions we also discussed the previous Sunday. Pastor Landahl sometimes argued with my tempos. I sometimes suggested he do something differently. We both confessed from time to time that we had chosen a wrong hymn, put it in the wrong place, or failed to consider how standing or sitting related to the congregation's singing. We listened to a tape of the service to check out our impressions. Then all of this information was utilized in future planning.

Sometimes we planned worship and analyzed it with a group of lay people. The ground rules for them were the same as for us. We all were disciplined by the lectionary and the propers. None of us got to choose just a few favorite hymns. Hymns had to fit the Sunday just like everything else we planned. These sessions with lay persons were quite rewarding and meaningful. They helped the pastor prepare sermons, helped me choose music, and helped us all understand worship more fully. They also kept the pastor and me from losing touch with the concerns of the people.

My own planning began with the people's song. The first issue was what the people would sing and how the organ or choir would lead them. My practice and the choir's practice all began there also—that is, with the hymns and the liturgy. Then I moved to propers and anthems for the choir and finally to separate organ or other instrumental music. The first and most critical thing was the Lord's song as it found expression among this specific people. Everything else worked from and related to that.

When I came to Ascension, the congregation already knew the better part of two settings of the liturgy itself. In the years I was there, the congregation learned those settings better and experimented with two other settings (one in a jazz idiom), they learned to sing psalms without accompaniment, they became flexible and receptive to various ways of singing hymns and psalms and to various musical styles, and many of them expressed their gratitude to the pastor and me for the time we spent trying to allow worship to have its integrity among them. The choir, a delightful group, came to understand and to exercise their leadership role in worship not only by leading psalms and hymns, but by proper verses, simple anthems, complex anthems, even in aleatory style, and a Bach cantata. We used many different instrumental soloists and ensembles, most characteristically in connection with hymn-singing, though for anthems and voluntaries as well.

Problems attended the organ for years, long before I came. One of my responsibilities was to help the congregation solve those problems. After much reading by a number of people, many visits to other churches and other organs, and careful meetings by committees and the whole church, the congregation voted to purchase a new organ. They decided to place it against the front wall under the rose window where the altar had been located, which put it on the center axis of the building so that it could speak with presence into the room to support congregational singing. The congregation also voted to renovate the worship space so that the altar and pulpit would be at the crossing. (The church is cruciform in design with two transepts. The balcony is small, so the rear of the church was not a possibility for the organ.) When the renovation was completed, we physically gathered around Word and Sacrament—the people on three sides, the organ and choir on the fourth. Decisions about the renovation and the organ were all made with worship in mind, not recitals or concerts. The people's song was always one of the central issues. Serious and careful consideration was given to many possibilities. The solution represented painstaking sifting and sorting by many people. It more than repaid the long hours of labor spent making the decision. The organ does what we hoped it would—leads the people in song. And the worship space is dynamic.

None of what Ascension did was due solely or even mostly to my role as its cantor. It was due to a community of faith of which both pastor and cantor were a part, struggling to find what it means to worship and sing the Lord's song in the late twentieth century in metropolitan Chicago. If you visited the church when Pastor Landahl and I were serving it, you would have found the congregational or choral singing excellent sometimes, less than excellent at others. Sometimes things clicked perfectly, and sometimes they were not so good—probably just like your parish. We were by no means perfect, and we were not qualitatively different from most other normal churches. If we were at all different from most, it was because we did indeed plan our worship in the hope that its integrity would not be assaulted by unplanned schizoid confusion. And we did sing the Lord's song.

I am a bit different perhaps from some church musicians across the country in that I have thought and studied more than many of them about the role of the church musician. I am also a seminary graduate and an ordained Lutheran pastor with responsibilities for Word and Sacrament, which are not common to most church musicians. But in other respects I am the same. For Ascension and the other churches I have served as musician, I have done the best I can with my moderate abilities and the limited time and resources of my place to help a specific portion of the body of the baptized sing the song they have been given. Like other church musicians I feel called to this vocation, like them I suffer disappointments, like them I share many joys, and like them I simply love what I do.[1]

That's what I wrote for the first edition of this book, except that I have cast it into the past tense. In 1990 I moved from Chicago, Illinois, to St. Paul, Minnesota, to become Professor of Church Music at Luther Seminary. I now serve as cantor for the Seminary community, teach courses about church music and worship, and administer the Master of Sacred Music (MSM) degree program offered by Luther Seminary in conjunction with St. Olaf College.

---

1. See "Journal of Church Music Reader Survey, Part II: The Readers Talk Back," *Journal of Church Music* 28: 4 (April 1986), 18–19. This article reports that when asked, "what is your greatest pleasure as a church musician?" the "responses . . . were virtually unanimous: most of you simply loved what you do!"

When I accepted the position at Luther, I had to give up all weekly Sunday responsibilities as musician or pastor because I needed to be free to visit the MSM students in their field work churches. (The MSM degree is intended to prepare church musicians who are trained at the master's level both theologically and musically. As part of their degree requirements, they must serve a church as a musician.) I have worked as a church musician in a local parish almost continuously since high school, so having no leadership responsibilities on Sunday was shocking at first, like being a fish out of water. I have gradually gotten used to it—and learned from it.

Though I had weekly responsibilities on Sundays in the churches I was serving, I had nonetheless over the years managed to find ways to visit numerous other churches in many different traditions, both by myself and with students in worship classes I have taught. These visits, coupled with the ones I now make to my students, have continuously confirmed ever more strongly what I wrote in the first edition of this book. Up to now this second edition is largely the same as the first, therefore, with only minor alterations. I have not changed my mind. If anything, I am more convinced about what I wrote the first time around. Since I wrote it, however, attacks on the church's worship, church music, and church musicians have become increasingly hostile, so two additional chapters need to be added.

Chapter 10

Challenges

IN RECENT YEARS, THE CHURCH'S WORSHIP has been attacked as not hospitable, not user-friendly, not seeker-friendly, and not conducive to evangelism. Church music and church musicians have borne the brunt of this attack. If you are or plan to be involved in church music at this point in our history, be prepared for challenges and conflict. In this chapter I will try to sort out what seem to me to be the issues.

We who are church musicians, it is true, are the point persons for much of this attack, and we can easily be made the scapegoats; however, we need to be careful not to shoulder too much responsibility for the current state of affairs. Far broader currents than musical ones are at work.

Broader Currents

One is the disappearance of more "informal" evening services and other meeting times throughout the week so that impossible attempts are now made to pack everything into a single hour on Sunday morning. Another is an attack on Word and Sacrament themselves. A third is the church's now habitual abdication of its role of doing theology, giving this role to academicians and thereby reducing "vital Christian piety to propositions."[1] Fourth,

---

1. Harmon L. Smith, *Where Two or Three Are Gathered: Liturgy and the Moral Life* (Cleveland: The Pilgrim Press, 1995), 2.

in spite of the truth of the previous point, "mainline" churches nevertheless have been identified with some forms of academic theology which, in response to cultural challenges, can be understood to use the word "God" to refer not to the living God of the Christian tradition, but to a projection of humanity's highest longings.[2] The practical result has been to make the complexity of the faith suspicious to some people and to drive them away from mainline churches to places where they are willing to accept more simplistic answers so long as the being of God is not obliterated. A fifth current is rampant biblical illiteracy. A sixth is that it's "cool" to be spiritual, but not "cool" to be part of an organized, especially mainstream, church. Seventh, the illusion of consensus by sincerity after the Second World War has turned out to be the mirage it was. North American gifts of diversity have been converted into polarization and meanness, and many churches have bought into such a spirit.

Little or nothing from this list is directly about music or musicians at all, though it clearly effects them. Church musicians should not try to shoulder blame for these realities, nor should we be tempted to view everything negatively, as I will say later. High-level historical currents are at work here, and musicians are not in control of them.

The Attack on Church Music

The part of the attack that relates to church music goes something like this: The organ, it is said, is outmoded, disliked by some congregations, foreign to the non-church-going public, and is without organists to play it or students interested in learning to play it. Further, church music is "classical," and only a small slice of the population is interested in "classical" music. Statistics are quoted to show how mainline churches are declining, how baby boomers find practices such as confessions of sins a "downer" (or baby busters or Generation X are repelled by them or attracted to

---

2. See Carl E. Braaten, "Scripture, Church, and Dogma: An Essay on Theological Method," *Interpretation: A Journal of Bible and Theology*, 51:2 (April 1996), 142–155.

something else), and how "classical" church music is a major culprit in keeping people away from church.

Churches that have accepted these presuppositions have organized "alternative" or "contemporary" worship services.[3] In such services small bands that are ubiquitous in the night clubs, late night television talk shows, and garages of our society have often replaced organs and choirs, sometimes replete with sexy lead singers, back-up vocalists, lots of electronic equipment, microphones, and a forthright attempt to entertain. The music of these groups can vary from rock to country western to warmed-over styles recently popular in the culture, and may have praise choruses or "teeny hymns" associated with them.[4] Sometimes anything written before 1970 is eschewed.

Perspective

Five broad points might be made before more specific responses are given in the next chapter. First, we need to be thankful for all the zeal and analytical work on our culture associated with some of the movements that seem to attack church music. People have made tabulations, assembled statistics, and tried to make sense of our period to speak the gospel to it. We can learn from all this material. We need to be careful about accuracy as in all analytical endeavors, but much of what is here can teach us many things.

Second, as long as a congregation gathers around Word and Sacrament and the music points beyond itself to God in Christ, style of worship and music can be considered irrelevant for Christians. In some sense, the labels "traditional" and "alternative" have become meaningless because they can be defined in such different ways. The deep structures of Word and Sacrament are sometimes more evident in "alternative" services than they are in "traditional" ones. A heavy metal mass, for example—

---

3. For my analysis of and response to this, see Paul Westermeyer, "Beyond 'Alternative' and 'Traditional' Worship," *The Christian Century* 109:10 (March 18–25), 300–302.

4. See George H. Shorney, *The Hymnal Explosion in North America* (Carol Stream: Hope Publishing Company, 1988), 7.

though it may be offensive and inappropriate to some—can use all the "traditional" elements of the mass, while a "traditional" service may have truncated the "tradition" into a quite untraditional affair. At the same time, some "alternative" or "contemporary" services are in theory constructed from scratch with a conscious contempt for the "tradition" and a view to Johnny Carson talk shows or later imitations as their model. They invariably call attention to those who lead them, not to God in Christ. Whatever the label, however, style is not the critical ingredient. Deeper realities are. Christians have done Word and Sacrament for two thousand years in many styles, in many languages, and with many kinds of music.

Third, there is room for experimentation and for many styles in the Christian church, and one always has to remember what Gamaliel, a teacher and respected Pharisee, told the high priest and council when they wanted to persecute Peter and the apostles:

> "Fellow Israelites, consider carefully what you propose to do to these men. . . . because if this plan or this undertaking is of human origin, it will fail; but if it is of God, you will not be able to overthrow them—in that case you may even be found fighting against God." (Acts 5:35b; 38b-39)

In time it always becomes clear what is of God and what is not.

Fourth, church musicians need to acknowledge their contributions to this situation. They have too often been elitists and have neglected the congregation's singing, while restricting their interests to concert repertoires, certain types of organs, or one period of literature. Concert repertoires and expertise about organs and literature are not bad at all. We need good performers and such expertise. But when they lead to contempt for the breadth of the church's song and especially for the singing of the people, there is big trouble. Musicians need to realize the trouble they have caused when they have forgotten the worshipers and their song.

At the moment, however, church musicians are less and less snobbish and are doing little or no persecuting. Many have bent over backwards in recent years trying to understand and use the new materials being proposed. (Many faithful church musicians have always done this.) I have lost track of the number of meetings and conferences in virtually every denomination, many of them extended over several days, which have attempted to address this topic as responsibly as possible.

Fifth, churches themselves need to own up to their contributions to the current situation. They have too often turned their worship life into ingrown, dry-as-dust habit which, at least as far as the world could perceive, had little if any vitality or life. They have failed to use their resources, have not planned or prepared for worship, have gotten stuck in narrow ruts of repetition, have reduced everything to one musical style and a few musical pieces, and have too often allowed leading the people's song and all the music around it to be reduced to appalling incompetence. The freedom of the church's liturgical life and worship's relation to the rest of life were often lost. Word and Sacrament and their explosive new life for the world were obscured or even forgotten. That God might have anything to do with this seemed altogether absent.

Church musicians and the churches they serve, though they need to own up to their sins, nevertheless now seem to be fair game for all sorts of attacks that go well beyond the bounds of any problems they have caused. This phenomenon especially characterizes "mainline" churches who have chosen self-loathing and trashing their own mothers and fathers as their program. Conference leaders of this new wave make fun of old people. They tell conferees to "go around" church musicians if they want anything really positive to happen in their churches, usually defined as numerical growth. A year or so before I left Elmhurst College, I got a call from someone who asked me as Music Department chair to provide him with musicians for a band he was starting so he could organize a new church which "would put all the churches in the western suburbs of Chicago out of business." In recent years I have received many phone calls from musicians and pastors all over the country,[5] many of whom I have never met, who are in pain because of things like this: At a conference of pastors, a leader of the church told the pastors to go home, instruct their organists to turn off their organs and turn on the synthesizers—and if the organists refuse, kill them. Or an electronic device with recordings of hymns is proposed as a substitute for organists, because pastors could control it and would not have to deal with musicians.

The new sectarianism and hostility that perspectives like this have created, especially within denominations and individual churches, are legion. One is loathe to enter the fray because the potential for ingrown arguing and forgetting the world we are called to serve is so great. But some things must be said precisely for the sake of the world. The next chapter is an attempt to say them.

5. Michael Hawn, who teaches at Southern Methodist University, tells me he too has received such calls, and that in 1992 in Dallas, several church musicians actually formed an ad hoc support group.

Chapter 11

Responses

Richness

THE CHRISTIAN FAITH IS SIMPLE. The small child can understand it. But genuine simplicity is rich and complex. Christian worship embodies that richness and complexity. To assume that what Christians have been doing for two thousand years in their worship could be easily accessible and immediately understandable to Christians themselves, much less to those outside the church, is absurd. That would suggest that the whole of life addressed by the gospel is not complex, that God's grace is not rich with meaning, and that there is no challenge and little substance to the Christian faith. Were that the case, Christianity would have evaporated from the face of the earth long ago. What we do in worship certainly should be friendly to the seeker, but to assume it can be thoroughly and immediately discernible to anyone is nonsense.

Statistics

Let us learn from the statistics, but not be controlled by them. As Gabriel Fackre points out, quoting Dietrich Bonhoeffer, Christians are not to be "servile before fact."[1] Their vision has to

---

1. Gabriel Fackre, "Common Calling and Confessing Christ" (computer script [1995]), 1.

do with new life in Christ, which is never identifiable with any cultural givens, statistical tabulations, or analyses of them.

Labels

While it is true that style is unimportant as long as the core of Word and Sacrament is present, there are dangers in labeling our worship. First, labels tend to call attention to what we do and miss the point of letting God's word have free course among us. Second, they mistakenly suggest we can dream up new liturgies (and ultimately make up the Christian faith as well). The result is to tyrannize people with leaders' idiosyncrasies. The value of the liturgy (about which there is a remarkable ecumenical consensus) is that it protects the people, protects their memory, and allows them to exercise their rightful office. That's why Martin Luther was so insistent that we not keep changing basic patterns because doing so leads to chaos and confusion.[2] Good worship is faithfulness to the church's historic underlying forms with enormous faithful freedom as well. Third, labels gear our worship to certain groups and split us into factions. The liturgy is not about taste or interest groups. It is not for one race or sex or generation or majority or minority or one anything. It is for all people. A critical struggle for our period is to learn how we can sing together. If history is any teacher, we will use both old and new, we who are church musicians will choose and compose by hearing with and for the people in the local churches we serve, and the church as a whole will encourage and commission the most skillful composers among us to give us our ears and our voices.

Children and Young People

One of the reasons worship is being labeled is that different styles are presumed to appeal to different age groups. Under that presupposition is another one, namely, that generational musical preferences ought to control us. It is true, of course, as people with

---

2. Martin Luther, "The German Mass and Order of Service, 1526," *Luther's Works, Volume 53: Liturgy and Hymns*, Ulrich S. Leupold, ed. (Philadelphia: Fortress Press, 1965), 80.

graded choir programs have known for years, that people like and comprehend different things at different stages in their development, that voices at different stages of development can do different things, and that different literature is therefore appropriate to different age groups. For example, doing Italian opera or English oratorios with high school students is probably not a good idea because their voices aren't ready for that repertoire.

However, children love to learn new things and usually do it much more quickly than adults. They can appreciate all styles of music and do amazing musical feats, as boy choirs—now sometimes girl, or boy and girl, choirs—have demonstrated for years and years. The professional boys or girls in these choirs compare with professional symphony musicians, and amateur young singers compare with amateur adult players and singers. Those who don't sing in choirs, young and old, appreciate being introduced to what they don't know.

The presupposition that we have to "dumb down"[3] our music or make one style of music for youth or any age group is nonsense. It's part of the logic that treats children (and adults) like objects. It uses and abuses music as a tool to manipulate them (and all the rest of us). Regarding children as cute things for adults to watch during children's sermons and then sending them into their own ghettos during the rest of the worship service are parts of this same notion that will, of course, lead to their leaving the church when they grow to be teenagers.[4]

Children, youth, the young, the middle-aged, the old, baby boomers, baby busters, and people in any other cohorts you want to create are not statistics. They are people who need to be treated with respect. Their likes and different developmental tasks must be respected, of course, but we all deserve to be treated well and stretched beyond our likes and dislikes, not pandered to.

---

3. This phrase is from Marva J. Dawn, *Reaching Out without Dumbing Down: A Theology of Worship for the Turn-of-the-Century Culture* (Grand Rapids: William B. Eerdmans Publishing Company, 1995).

4. See "Listen-Listen-Listen," in Brian Wren, *Piece Together Praise: A Theological Journey, Poems and Collected Hymns Thematically Arranged* (Carol Stream: Hope Publishing Company, 1996), 132.

"Stretching" can be another form of manipulation, to be sure, but that is not our current danger.

At worship we are called to be together around pulpit, font, and table. Worship is not about our personal or generational likes and ought not to be a replication of the society's divisions. In part it will be, of course, because the church participates in the world's brokenness. But the church is not in the business of affirming and contributing to that disease. It has another vision and another reality to embody—to present Christ and as one body of Christ to gather together beyond ourselves in Christ. Human beings of all age groups respond best to challenges and visions that lead them beyond their current states. The healthy church affirms its christological vision to be beyond all human visions. If the church loses that vision, it is like salt without saltiness.

Post-Christian

"Post-Christian" may be taken to mean many things. By it I mean that the structures of our culture don't support the Christian church and its message. They are not necessarily hostile to the church, but they don't support it either. Unlike the period between approximately the years 312 (Constantine's Peace of the Church) and 1776 (the American Revolution—or 1789, the French Revolution, if you prefer) in the West when the structures of the state supported the church and often were synonymous with it, we don't have such supports. For some people, especially Anabaptists, this is good. They often say that Constantine's support was the worst thing that could have happened to the church.

Whatever you may think about that particular issue, our situation may not actually be different from any other time. Regardless of the presence of nominal support, the Christian message always stands over the culture and subverts it. Further, as soon as the church thinks it and the culture are identifiable with one another, it is in trouble because Christianity has then lost its cruciform, servant character and has become triumphalist. But, whether our situation is actually different, it looks different to those who remember full churches in the abnormal bubble of the 1950s or in historical moments like the fourth, thirteenth, nineteenth, or some other century of choice, which the viewer perceives as a pristine age of cultural support and synthetic perfection.

There is the temptation to climb back into the cultural envelope to replicate some perceived past ideal synthesis. Clearly, however, you can't climb into some real or imagined past—with the music of nineteenth century confessional recoveries, nineteenth century gospel hymnody, chorales or psalm tunes from the sixteenth century, Renaissance polyphony, Bach harmonizations, Romanesque or Gothic architecture, or whatever—to create a cultural synthesis for our day. You'll get a museum piece. Some, therefore, would like to redo the cultural synthesis by climbing into our culture's skin with its market mentality, asking what people want, being controlled by needs and choices, making Christianity fit individualist and consumerist models, and using the culture's commercial music in the culture's commercial way. While this may seem to "work" momentarily, it has all the problems any past nostalgia has, turns out to be just one more museum piece, turns Christianity into an ideology, and substitutes one perversion for another. You get the dregs of the culture and not the vitality of the gospel.

Critiques and the Church Musician

We live in a period of flux, without any consensus. This lack of center stimulates critique and blame. From the right we are told the church does not care about things like evangelism, family values, prayer, or morality. So, some argue, we should scuttle the past and start from scratch with our own histories and music, usually defined in practice since about 1970. From the left we are told the church does not care about social justice, the poor, the dispossessed, women, and homosexuals. So, some argue, we should scuttle all the patriarchy, sexism, racism, homophobia and worship materials that go with them and start from scratch with new or radically altered texts, music, and structures.

The church musician is attacked from both sides, sometimes as the central culprit. No matter what the musician's personal commitments are, she or he realizes something is out of whack every time the past is forgotten, worship is collapsed either into evangelism or a social agenda, and music is used as a tool of control. When that happens, you lose the church's story and song, you lose both worship and the thing you try to collapse it into, and the song won't sing. In the process the musician's musical terrain, aesthetic sensitivity, creativity, music-making capacity, and practice time are all drained away. Polarization, hostility, and choosing up sides are forced, and the devil is loose: the very shalom that music provides is turned into its opposite.

The Past

The church over time counters any age's tendency to dismiss the past and presents another perspective that says the Holy Spirit is not only operative in the present, but has been at work in the past as well. To neglect the past witness is to imperil our own. We are not to be controlled by the past any more than we are to be controlled by the present. Both past and present have their deep fissures. But to neglect the past is to deny God's activity in it and to make us captive to our own versions of reality. "[I]n order to get our bearings, and from there to chart our course as Christians in our time and place, we need to understand our inheritance. Without it, we don't know who we are, where we come from, or where we are destined to go."[5]

Perspective

The current situation can be viewed as all negative: change, attacks, and hostility abound along with wicked people who love power and, at times of flux like ours, manage to terrorize and tyrannize others with more ease than usual. But all of that is simply the shape our version of the world's brokenness takes. That's the way it is and always has been. Things are always broken. Periods

---

5. Smith, *Where Two or Three Are Gathered*, 4.

of flux like ours are also fecund, however. Joseph Sittler's phrase, "the fecundity of the darkness," is an apt one. Such a time offers enormous opportunities to teach, to rethink, to learn, and to allow new possibilities to explode.

Further, the culture itself is not all bad. It offers incredible possibilities, enormously positive freedoms and choices, pockets of song that break out where you least expect them, surprising kindnesses. As at all times, we find a mix of things that includes wonder, joy, amazing opportunities, celebrations, and delights.

Cantors and pastors in partnership ought to be able to approach our world with the broadest picture of past and present and the most creativity under the umbrella of God's grace, then set their gifts to work singing the Christian faith into our period. For while it is true that the culture we live in has impeded and in many instances even stopped our song, humanity still longs to sing. To worship is to be, and to be human is to sing,[6] especially at worship. Church musicians are called to give us our voice.

Note what that means. The ideal music in any local church is not the concert or recorded music of Amy Grant, the Robert Shaw Chorale, the Beatles, the St. Olaf Choir, the Anonymous Four, or any other group or sound you might choose, which is imported from without, no matter how good or bad it may be. We should learn from any and all sounds, but the ideal music in a local church is the sound the people themselves make around Word and Sacrament. It is what the cantor leads and why the cantor is so important. To substitute external, extrinsic sounds for the sound of the people themselves is to contravene the very nature of the Christian worshiping community. It is the same as, maybe even worse than, piping in a sermon.

As always, the song of the people comes into being with a cantor—full-time, part-time, with more or less ability and training. Though this is one of the most exciting things a human being could do, many able and committed church musicians have bailed out because they have been treated so badly by the church.

---

6. See Paul Westermeyer, "To Be Human Is to Sing," *The Luther Northwestern Story*, 7:1, (Winter 1990), 4–8.

The church needs to encourage them and to pay them adequately for their labor.

Organs

You don't need an organ or any instruments at all in Christian worship. All you need are human voices.[7] But, if you're going to have an instrument, the pipe organ still works best. It fills large spaces with sound, makes sounds with air through pipes like the human voice, can therefore lead congregational singing better than any other instrument, and can produce multiple lines and various colors like an instrumental group with the advantage that the sounds are under one person's control. Second, the question of practicality cannot be avoided. For most churches it is more efficient and better stewardship for one person to practice than to attempt to get an instrumental group together week after week. Third, worship has more life and vitality if instruments and instrumental groups are used from time to time in various changing configurations rather than always. That does not suggest avoiding instruments or instrumental groups. I certainly want to use them—all kinds of them from orchestral and band instruments alone and in groups to Orff instruments to bells to Conga drums and other percussive pieces to synthesizers, etc.— quite often. It means breaking open texts with instrumental color is far more possible when those colors are used selectively rather than perpetually. Finally, one person can respond to the flow of a service in a way a group simply cannot. That is true even for those of us who improvise in the most elementary way. Virtually every worship service has moments when plans need to be modified. A sensitive organist can make the necessary adjustments. Even the most exceptional improvisatory instrumental group is hard-pressed to do the same thing as well.

---

7. Aidan Kavanagh, in typically trenchant language, says it well: "The human voice is the premier instrument in liturgical worship, and its basic repertoire is the psalms. Mechanical devices are secondary at best, and their various repertoires are frequently tangential to the assembly's liturgical purpose." Aidan Kavanagh, *Elements of Rite: A Handbook of Liturgical Style* (New York: Pueblo Publishing Company, 1982), 32.

The church has a long history of working out its relationship with the organ. The organ has a repertoire more deeply connected with the Christian faith than any other instrument, in all kinds of styles. That fact alone suggests its teaching and evangelical value. When the literature is played well on real organs and used appropriately, almost everybody loves it—in spite of what we are being told to the contrary. The church will rediscover the pipe organ when the current hostilities have subsided. One hopes it will happen before a void is created and the church's current self-hatred has done too much damage (not only to music and musicians).

A final comment needs to be added. There are more organists and people interested in the organ than is admitted. If we lock up organs and don't let students practice on them, if we attack organs and do everything possible to discourage children who are fascinated by them, and if we pay organists slave wages or abuse them, of course we won't have them.

Microphones

Microphones are part and parcel of our culture. Like anything human beings have created, they can be used well or poorly. In congregational singing where they intrinsically grow out of the sound of the people, as in some African American and charismatic groups, they work. They can easily imperil congregational singing when they are extrinsic to it, however, because they give leaders sounds people cannot imitate. It is no accident that churches where leaders sing through microphones often turn congregations to silence. In most situations microphones have to be used judiciously or not at all if you want good congregational song. This is one of the reasons Alice Parker (who often leads hymns with just her voice), John Bell (from the Iona Community who does the same), Ken Nafziger and Mary Oyer (gifted Mennonite leaders of congregational song) avoid microphones and why the singing they empower is so much more vigorous than singing by leaders with microphones.

I have indicated earlier how critical acoustics are to congregational singing. Importing microphones is sometimes attempted to repair the damage of poor acoustics in order to give the impression of reverberation. This imitative sound is not genuine, so it denies the honest spirit of Christian worship. Further, it is for leaders' voices only and leaves out the congregation and its voice.

Placement of Musicians

Because entertainment is a large part of the control, some people are arguing to move musicians—from rear galleries, for example—to places where they can be seen. Two comments need to be made.

First, musicians who are seen can help lead worship services, but seeing them can turn into regarding them as entertainers. When that happens the essence of worship has been undone. Second, there is no single place in worship spaces for musicians and instruments. The church has employed a variety of placements. We would be well-advised, however, not to be too quick to alter spaces where musicians are above the congregation in a rear gallery. It is one of the best places for leading congregational singing, and it avoids calling attention to the musicians who themselves join the rest of the congregation around the central focus of Word and Sacrament.

Misconceptions

Recurring misconceptions have become axiomatic. Faulty assertions are assumed to be true and then used as arguments for whatever one wants to do, usually in what is mistakenly called a "popular" vein. Whether these misconceptions support choosing certain kinds of music in our worship is itself open to question, but at the very least we need to get the record straight. Here are some of these misleading axioms.

1. *Luther said, "Why should the devil have all the good tunes?"* I'm not sure what this would prove if Luther said it, especially considering what he might have meant by "good" or "the devil." "Good" may not have referred to "popular," and "the devil" may

have meant the pope or the church of Rome. But that's a moot point. So far as Carl Schalk (who has read everything Luther wrote about music) and others of us who have searched can tell, Luther didn't say this.[8]

2. *John Wesley said, "Why should the devil have all the good tunes?"* Again, it's not clear to me what this would indicate if he said it, but where did he say it? Carlton Young has assembled a thorough-going overview of the Wesleys' thoughts about music. He says "there is no evidence he [John] used this phrase to justify using a variety of music." He cites Nicholas Temperley and Frank Baker as

> narrowing the source of this oft-quoted phrase to E. W. Broome's book published in 1881, on the Anglican clergyman Rowland Hill, 1744–1833, a critic of John Wesley. Broome says of Hill, "He did not see any reason why the devil should have all the good tunes." [9]

Curiously enough, in an undocumented story, a sixteenth century Roman Catholic priest, presumably one of Luther's critics, also said this (and Charles Wesley and General William Booth, among others)! There is much fiction here, and it proves nothing.

3. *Luther raided the bars for his hymn tunes.* I'm not sure what a barroom tune would be nor what knowing one would prove, but it certainly is not true.[10] (It's also not true that Luther used simple or "alternative" liturgies.[11]) Luther followed the Minne-

---

8. Cf. Calvin Stapert, "Beyond Cheap Thrills," *Perspectives* 8: 9 (November 1993), 3.

9. Carlton R. Young, *Music of the Heart: John and Charles Wesley on Church Music and Musicians* (Carol Stream: Hope Publishing Company, 1995), 104.

10. See David Music, "Getting Luther out of the Barroom," *The Hymn* 45: 4 (October 1994), 51; Johannes Riedel, *The Lutheran Chorale: Its Basic Traditions* (Minneapolis: Augsburg Publishing House, 1967); and *Luther's Works, Volume 53: Liturgy and Hymns*.

11. See Forum Letter 25:6 (June 1996), 2: "Luther's 'simple liturgies' are not simple. His liturgical reforms were sensibly conservative. If conducted today as in Luther's time, the Deutsche Messe would look like a medieval high mass compared to the real simplicity available in the Lutheran Book of Worship. The Deutsche Messe comes complete with chant for pastors, antiphons by choir, directions for creed to be sung, instructions to elevate host and cup during the German

singers and Meistersingers and used *Barform*, a German word that means a poem with more than one stanza, each stanza in the form AAB. It has nothing to do with bars in the sense of pubs. Luther's sources were Gregorian chant, medieval vernacular hymns, and two secular folk melodies, which didn't have staying power and themselves were abandoned for new tunes. If anything, Luther can be accused of not using popular music. His characteristic metrical version of the *Sanctus* is anything but a bar tune, whatever that is.[12] Erik Routley, the twentieth century's foremost hymnologist, had this to say:

> Certain slanders aimed at Luther have some truth in them, but none have [sic] less than the rumour that he adapted 'popular music' for use with his hymns. He wrote his texts on the outward form of the ballads and art-songs which appealed to the top layers of society—the liveliest and most ingenious, not the easiest and most elementary music of his time.[13]

Luther united old and new, high art and folk art, rural and urban in two ways: 1) by the chorale itself and 2) by the practice of alternating—one stanza the monophonic and unaccompanied folk-like song of the people in the chorale, the next stanza the high art of trained groups singing and/or playing a polyphonic setting. It should be added that the distinction between sacred and secular was not nearly so strong for Luther as for us, but he did distinguish what was appropriate to worship.[14]

4. *John Wesley raided the bars for his hymn tunes.* If he did, they're not the ones that had staying power. None of the tunes

---

Sanctus, plus a number of other things that would appear pointlessly ceremonial to today's Lutheran and even to post-Vatican II Roman Catholics. Luther's earlierrevision of the mass, the Formula Missae (where he retained Latin), in many ways is even more imposing."

12. *Lutheran Book of Worship* (Minneapolis: Augsburg Publishing House, 1978), hymn 528.

13. Erik Routley, *Christian Hymns Observed* (Princeton: Prestige Publications, Inc., 1982), 18.

14. See *Luther's Works, Volume 53: Liturgy and Hymns*, 306.

that Wesley himself chose, which are in the current Methodist hymnal, fits the description.[15] The closest thing one can find to a "bar tune" is described by Carlton Young as follows.

> [A] pub tune (folk melody) was central to Charles Wesley's writing "the True Use of Musik." According to Frank Baker . . . , the text was probably composed to the tune "Nancy Dawson," similar to "Here we go 'round the mulberry bush," and sung in response to a company of half-drunken sailors who had interrupted Charles's open-air preaching service in Plymouth, 1746.[16]

Here is part of the text Charles Wesley wrote for that tune.

> Listed into the Cause of Sin,
>   Why should a Good be Evil?
> Musick, alas! too long has been
>   Prest to obey the Devil:
>
> Who on the Part of God will rise
>
> Musick in Virtue's Cause retain,
>   Rescue the Holy Pleasure?[17]

A few observations are in order. First, Young's parenthesis "folk melody" for "pub tune" is probably the closest one can get to a definition. Second, the specific tune employed is something like "Here we go 'round the mulberry bush." If that defines "bar tune," we need to ask if it's really what we want as steady fare for our worship. Third, this hymn was for a very specific situation and not put forward as a general principle for worship. Fourth, maybe here is another place where the "devil" business comes from. Note, however, that the question is not "Why should the devil have all the good tunes?" It is the use to which music as a whole is put.

John Wesley's position about music goes something like this:[18] He was worried about "vain repetitions" and did not like ei-

---

15. Young, 55, lists the tunes, all of which have churchly sources: AMSTERDAM, CARREY'S (SURREY), EASTER HYMN, HANOVER, OLD 113TH, SAVANNAH, TALLIS' CANON, UFFINGHAM, VATER UNSER, WER NUR DEN LIEBEN GOTT.

16. Young, 170.

17. Ibid.

18. See Young, especially 84–105.

ther repeated choruses or polyphony. He thought modern harmony drained music of its more primal monophonic power,
though he was attracted to Handelian opera and eighteenth century tunes with figured bass.[19] Reminiscent of Plato, he thought
singing too many hymns back to back enervated or enfeebled
rather than strengthened a community. In short, neither those who
advocate high art or popular music get much support from John
Wesley. He would not take kindly to repeated choruses, to piling
up a whole series of praise choruses or hymns one after the other,
or to polyphonic pieces.

Routley summarized "the Methodist doctrine of hymnody"
as follows:

> Give us the best music we can have, but make it
> *friendly* to the people. . . . Wesleyan hymnody was
> more democratic than Calvin or even Luther because
> in proportion as its more hospitable theology admit-
> ted the capacity of all things for redemption it was
> able to make greater use of the secular idiom. But it
> shared with the universal church the conviction that
> music acts upon the singer with an effect correspond-
> ing in benefit to the integrity of the music.[20]

Young's summary goes this way:

> Wesley is the paradigmatic enabler of that brand of
> vital congregational song that combines the singable,
> the heartfelt, and the appropriate—a repertory that
> since his time has often been the enigma and some-
> times the nemesis of clergy and church musician
> alike.[21]

Young defines "popular music for Wesley's educated con-
stituents" as "the arias and occasional music of opera and orato-
rio, the broadsheet ballad . . . and the parlor song, folk music

---

19. There are contradictions in Wesley's thought. See Young, 89–91, especially
points 2 and 9.

20. Erik Routley, *The Church and Music: An Enquiry into the History, the Nature,
and the Scope of Christian Judgment on Music* (London: Gerald Duckworth & Co.
Ltd., 1950), 161.

21. Young, 113.

combined with dance, and concerts."[22] No bar tunes here, whatever they are.

5. *Classical music is used to keep the riffraff out of the church.* For
congregational singing, "classical music" means a wealth of
things that includes the congregational stratum of Gregorian
chant, Lutheran chorales, Genevan Psalter tunes, the music of the
Oxford movement, white spirituals, black spirituals, and Welsh
tunes. All of that music did just the opposite of this assertion,
namely, invited the riffraff in. Historically, classical hymn tunes
have not kept the riffraff out.

If "classical" means Ludwig van Beethoven, as it often
seems to, one wonders how it applies to church music. There is
resistance in our culture to the classical tradition for which
Beethoven stands, certainly. Apart from the tune HYMN TO JOY,
however, which was taken from his Ninth Symphony and which,
contrary to the general wisdom, unchurched people seem to
know and like, Beethoven has little to do with church music.

I have never known anyone who left the church because the
quality of its music was too "classical" or too fine. I have met numerous priests, pastors, and lay people who as "riffraff children"
joined the church through an excellent choir or were sustained by
"classical" music when their faith was weak. I have also met people who left the church because the quality of its music was too
poor or not "classical" enough, and there are people who joined
the church because they were attracted by superficial music and
then left when they couldn't stand a steady diet of it any more.

This statement is really one of contempt for those of us
who come from the riffraff, like me from a family of German im-
migrants who struggled with little money for several generations and my best friend in high school from a large,
low-income, African American family. It assumes the church has
nothing to offer people except what will presumably attract us
in whatever state we happen to be. My friend and I found
churches that eschewed the "classical" tradition and tried to at-

---

22. Young, 104.

tract people with low quality superficiality to be extremely offensive.

This assertion is untrue theologically. Great "classical"
music and art are for everybody. There is no riffraff. That's the
message of the Christian faith and the reality of the great art the
church has inevitably stimulated. That's why it is precisely the
poor riffraff in the slums who object when their beautiful old
church with its stained glass windows and organ are to be torn
down. That's why you find young and old, rich and poor, hetero-
and homosexual, men and women, sane and crazy, healthy and
unhealthy, and people of various ethnic backgrounds all together
in the great cathedrals of large cities where there is the finest
"classical" art and music.

The gospel requires that we treat one another well—with
the highest possible care, love, and respect. Great art does that—
for everybody. We are all riffraff; in Christ none of us is riffraff.
"Once you were no people, but now you are God's people" (1
Peter 2:10a; see also Rom. 9:25–26). We all deserve the best of
both high art and folk art. That's the classical tradition, and it in-
vites us all in.

What lies behind the notion that classical music keeps the
riffraff out is a false dichotomy between high and low culture. On
the high culture side it takes the form of "guarding" something—
like high culture or the faith or certain "classics." Christianity says
there's nothing to guard. You speak the Word into this wonderful
but cracked world, treat people well with no manipulation or
commercial control, craft the finest music to clothe the Word in all
styles for all people with love, and let the chips fall where they
may. As I will shortly say again, the issues that relate to music are
durability, honesty, and treating people well; not high or low culture or classical or folk art or any other stream you want to invent.
What the human race has done that is beautiful in high art and
folk art, from a Penderecki Passion to a spiritual, is for all of us.

6. *Church musicians are only concerned with music, not with
Jesus Christ.* It's true that some church musicians are more concerned with music than with Jesus Christ. It's also true that some

clergy are more concerned with power and control than they are with Jesus Christ, and some lay people are more concerned with status than with Jesus Christ. If we're going to attack musicians for their misplaced loyalties, then let's be honest and note that neither they nor anybody else has a corner on faith or its absence. And let's also be aware that the church includes all sorts and conditions of humanity in all states of development and pilgrimage. Presuming that everybody in the church will always have high octane faith is to be blind to theological and historical reality. The sun and the Son shine on the just and the unjust, the wheat and the tares grow up together in the church, and musicians are as subject to these realities as everybody else. All of us, not just musicians, need to be challenged to be faithful in our ministries.

Mostly, this proves nothing about what music we are to use. We're flirting here with Donatism, a fourth century African schism, which Augustine opposed. The church, taking Augustine's position, learned that sacraments are valid even if the minister who administers them is unworthy. That is, God is active and faithful whether we are worthy or not (and we're all always unworthy).

Music is not a sacrament (though it may be sacramental), but there is a parallel here. Just because a musician is unworthy has nothing to do with whether a certain kind of music ought to be used. A good deed by a prostitute is not rendered invalid because a prostitute did it. We have to make judgments for everything, including music, on grounds other than our worthiness.

7. *Since people in our society don't sing, sing for them with a band and singers.* That's fine if you want to replicate the Middle Ages when the people were silent spectators, but Vatican II had something else to say about the importance of the people's participatory singing in worship. So do those standing in the heritage of the sixteenth century Reformers who were concerned for the priesthood of all believers, which meant in part that the people have an office in worship, and they express it in their song. (Ulrich Zwingli, who ruled out all music, is an exception.) Neither priest nor priestly choir/band nor anyone else does it for

them. Some churches will argue, legitimately I think, that sometimes congregations should listen actively to a choir sing a text
on their behalf, but that can never be a general principle for all
the church all the time.

Let us also note, while it is true that white people in the
middle-class consumer culture often do not sing, some minorities
in our society sing with vigor at their worship services: some
African Americans, some people from Spanish-speaking cultures, some Pentecostals, some Moravians, some Mennonites,
some German or Scandinavian or Slovakian Lutherans, some
Presbyterians, some Methodists, some Congregationalists, some
Roman Catholics (yes, even some Roman Catholics!), etc. We
might learn from them rather than be controlled by the culture's
model of silence. Every Christian congregation in the country has
within it the seeds of congregational song. The church's best instincts are to water them, not stamp them out.

Specificity

How then does the Christian cantor, the church musician, approach her or his task in this situation? Pretty much the same as
the faithful cantor in all periods has done. You have to choose
and compose things for congregations to sing, so you make a
grid of questions, such as: Is it well-constructed so it's worth the
people's time and effort? Is it congregational? Can the people
make sense of it? Do the words say what we mean to say? Is the
text inclusive? Does it fit the flow of the service? Is there balance
in a given service, balance over a season or a year, and balance in
the full biblical story and use of the Psalms?

Texts need to be good poetry, "friendly to the people," as Erik
Routley might say—neither a Shakespearean sonnet nor a nursery
rhyme. Ambrose, Clement Marot, Martin Luther, Isaac Watts,
Charles Wesley, John Mason Neale, Catherine Winkworth, and the
contemporary writers in *With Tongues of Fire*[23] are good examples.

---

23. Paul Westermeyer, *With Tongues of Fire: Profiles in 20th-Century Hymn
Writing* (St. Louis: Concordia Publishing House, 1995).

For both music and texts we need to use:

- the *old* and the *new*. The old helps us keep pace with our sisters and brothers who have sung the song before us and keeps for our children things they may understand better than we do. The new helps us live into our time with its melody and rhythms.

- the *parochial* and the *catholic*. The parochial, that which comes from our specific place, helps us sing in the language of our people. The catholic helps us hear that the faith extends beyond us and helps the nomads of our society when they move around. The terms "ethnic" and "multicultural" could be used here, but they are now so misused and misunderstood that they have often become useless.

- the *simplest* to the most *complex*. These words need to be applied and made appropriate to a specific group. What is complex for one church may not be complex for another. But an enormous range of music is out there, to fit all of our various capacities and to reflect the richness of the faith. Another way of stating this distinction is folk song and high art.

- the *priestly* and the *prophetic*. God comforts and afflicts, consoles and judges. The words and music of the faith need to reflect that reality. If everything is a sweet saccharine bubble, the faith is distorted, just as if everything is an angular and jagged dissonance.

When dealing specifically with the music of the congregation, the *first* consideration is to avoid long rests, or what amounts to the same thing, long tied notes. Congregations can't count measures of silence or held notes and then come in on fractions of beats.

Second, the style has to be congregational, that is, folk-like, not soloistic. Much of the music of our culture is solo music and won't work for congregational singing. What is overly emotive won't work either, partly because the more emotive it is the more soloistic it is, but partly also because overly emotive can mean in-group and not welcoming. The hymnody of the church is sometimes criticized for being an in-group activity. That's a fair criticism, similar to the perspective of C. S. Lewis who regarded hymnody as the gang songs of the church. But you don't solve the problem by over-emoting (and usually avoiding good craft in the process); that solution increases the problem, because it makes hymn singing more closed to those outside the emotive circle. Congregational song is folk-like, with a hardy and welcoming character.

Third, augmented and diminished intervals, major sixths, and sevenths are problems in congregations' melody lines. With the exceptions of tunes that outline and prepare them carefully and support them with a clear harmonic structure, avoid such intervals if you want your congregation to sing.

Fourth, the tunes you use have to gravitate to a tonal or modal center. As Béla Bartók discovered when he did his research in the Balkans, an atonal folk melody is impossible.

Fifth, tunes may be multi-metric or syncopated, like the original form of the tune for "A Mighty Fortress" or the Jamaican tune LINSTEAD, which is used for "Let Us Talents and Tongues Employ," but, like these examples, patterns must be in a folk-like idiom so human beings who don't practice before services can do them.

Sixth, ranges and tessituras have to be where normal human beings can sing. Climax and anticlimax notes can push the range, but you can't transpose pieces up or down to some place where a given soloist happens to feel comfortable. Nor can you group most notes of a melody below middle C or above the next C up and expect congregations to sing.

Seventh, texts of strophic music should have the syllables structured the same way for every stanza. Soloists and choirs can add or subtract syllables and put more or fewer notes on the same syllable from stanza to stanza, but congregations will almost always have problems. Hymnody is a very disciplined business. Exercising its discipline is one of the ways cantors treat their congregations well.

Finally, a good test for a piece of congregational music is whether it can stand alone without accompaniment. That does not mean accompaniments are bad or should not be used, though we usually are afraid to give the people their voice alone and should do it more often. It means the genre that is endemic to a congregation's song is what the congregation can do alone. The more a piece depends upon an accompaniment, the less congregational it is likely to be.

Presuppositions

Obviously some presuppositions are at work here. One presupposition is that what we use needs to be durable and well-crafted; what we can grow into, not out of; what will serve us well as children and on our death-bed. This guideline does not suggest the Romantic notion of composing for eternity; it implies good craft that treats people with the same respect and concern God does. Of course there is a place for the throw-away, but it's not the central feature or control. The song was there before we were born, it will be there long after we are dead, and the church musician's vocation is in part to sort out what is worth the church's time and effort over the long haul. The church itself will do the sorting whether we like it or not. It will only keep what is worth keeping. The body has different members, and the church musician's role in the body is partly to save the church some time and do the sorting for them. Yes, the church musician will make mistakes in the process, like all human beings make mistakes. But with love for the people, innate abilities, and training in the discipline of church music, the cantor is in the best position to figure out this sorting task with empathy.

Another presupposition is honesty. The music the cantor chooses and the way she or he uses it must have integrity and be neighborly. Music and its use cannot be intended to manipulate. Manipulation is tyranny, and, of all people, those of us who live in our century ought to know about that.

A third presupposition is that we have to deal fundamentally with the congregation's singing. From that, choirs and instrumental groups and all manner of richly textured music-making grow, with and without professionals.

Finally, the musician must be musical. Being musical means such things as phrasing that breathes; introductions and consistent spacing between stanzas of a hymn to make it clear when a congregation is to begin singing; tempos that fit the particular piece, the time, the place, the people, the season; dynamics that are neither too quiet nor too loud all the time, but use the whole spectrum as is appropriate.

The Spirit of the Age

Clearly, the spirit of our age is to define Christianity by means of the culture around us. Musically this definition means using commercial jingles. More broadly it means adopting the culture's commercial point of view and making Christianity into one more product to be sold. Of course the church will adapt music of the culture. There is no alternative. The problem here is adopting it as a sales pitch. Christianity has nothing to sell. It announces new life for the taking. A secondary but no less serious problem is the one Don Saliers identifies by pointing to "William Inge's observation that the church that marries the spirit of an age becomes a widow in the next generation."[24] That is what we are flirting with, a spiritual ecology or lack thereof, which will leave our children high and dry and which, in spite of all the euphemistic talk about evangelism, will yield the next generation an evangelical disaster with truly empty churches.

Church musicians are among those whose gifts and vocation should enable them to see beyond the moment, to help the church avoid such a disaster, to love our culture and sing into it now, and to know better than to collapse everything into the present moment so that the song and its vitality will still be viable for the future.

I hope this book stimulates new insights and coherences for many of you in order to help you in this task. I hope you will hang in there by God's grace with a healthy perspective no matter how much you are attacked, because both church and world need you. And I wish you the shalom of the church's song.

Soli Deo Gloria!

Annotated Bibliography

THE FOLLOWING BOOKS PROVIDE a sampling of resources available to the cantor. When individual cantors cannot afford to buy them, churches could consider including them in their libraries. Resources of this sort are valuable not only to the cantor, but to the whole church.

Apart from the Bible, the most valuable book for any cantor is the hymnal. It has an array of material for both the study and practice of the church's worship and song. The second most valuable book for the cantor is the companion to the hymnal. Most denominational hymnals have quite respectable companions plus a wide array of additional materials related to the hymnal and worship.[1] For those that do not, other companions can be substituted. Though they are not geared to one's own hymnal, so many hymns and service materials are common to all standard hymnals that much information can be transferred. Since both hymnals and companions are for individual denominations through whom they can easily be acquired, they are not listed here.

---

1. For Lutherans, for example, the Association of Lutheran Church Musicians has assembled a *Guide to Basic Resources for the Lutheran Church Musician* (St. Louis: MorningStar Music Publishers, 1995).

The following list is more general. It includes liturgical, musical, and theological resources. Some of the theological resources are likely to be in many pastors' libraries.

The Anchor Bible Dictionary. Edited by David Noel Freedman. New York: Doubleday, 1992. A six-volume encyclopedia that identifies and explains biblical names, terms, and subjects.

Barth, Karl. *Dogmatics in Outline*. New York: Harper & Brothers, 1959. A brief overview of the Christian faith, organized according to the Apostles' Creed, by a Reformed theologian.

Benson, Louis F. *The English Hymn*. Richmond: John Knox Press, 1915, reprinted 1962. A classic history of English psalmody and hymnody, written in a somewhat wordy way.

Blume, Friedrich, et al. *Protestant Church Music: A History*. New York: W. W. Norton & Company, Inc., 1974. Most of this massive history first appeared in German in 1964 as *Geschichte der Evangelischen Kirchenmusik*.

Copyright: The United States Copyright Law, A Guide for Church Musicians. Church Music Publishers Association, P.O. Box 4329, Washington, D.C., 20012.

Copyright Law Basics. Single sheet available from Augsburg Fortress, P.O. Box 1209, Minneapolis, Minnesota 55440-1209; 612/330-3398 or 800/421-0239.

Costen, Melva Wilson. *African American Christian Worship*. Nashville: Abingdon Press, 1993. An overview from a Presbyterian perspective.

The New Westminster Dictionary of Liturgy and Worship. Edited by J. G. Davies. Philadelphia: The Westminster Press, 1986. Extended definitions of terms related to worship, updated from an edition in 1972.

Dawn, Marva J. *Reaching Out without Dumbing Down: A Theology of Worship for Turn-of the-Century Culture*. Grand Rapids: William B. Eerdmans, 1995. Thoughtful analysis of our current situation.

English Language Liturgical Consultation. *Praying Together*. Nashville: Abingdon Press, 1988. Common liturgical texts with emendations and annotations.

Eskew, Harry, and Hugh T. McElrath, *Sing with Understanding: An Introduction to Christian Hymnody*. 2d ed., revised and expanded. Nashville: Church Street Press, 1995. A new edition of this overview of the history of hymnody with practical suggestions.

Fackre, Gabriel. *The Christian Story: A Narrative Interpretation of Basic Christian Doctrine*, vol. I. Grand Rapids: William B. Eerdmans Publishing Company, 1996, first published 1978. The Christian faith with its major themes explained as story in and for the contemporary world.

———. *The Christian Story: A Pastoral Systematics*, vol. II. Grand Rapids: William B. Eerdmans, Publishing Company, 1987. More intensive study than the overview of volume I and geared more to pastors, but helpful for musicians as well.

Faulkner, Quentin. *Wiser Than Despair: The Evolution of Ideas in the Relationship of Music and the Christian Church*. Westport: Greenwood Press, 1996. A detailed yet broad historic overview which explores what the subtitle says.

Foley, Edward, Capuchin. *Ritual Music: Studies in Liturgical Musicology*. Beltsville, MD: The Pastoral Press, 1995. An ongoing conversation with a bibliographical overview, studies in the early church and the complexity of the cantor, Martin Luther, and later Roman Catholic thought.

Gelineau, Joseph. *Voices and Instruments in Christian Worship*. Translated by Clifford Howell. Collegeville: The Liturgical Press, 1964. A thoughtful and complete overview of the principles and applications of music in the Roman Catholic Church.

Hageman, Howard G. *Pulpit and Table*. Richmond: John Knox Press, 1962. A brief, easy-to-read history of Reformed worship.

Halter, Carl, and Carl Schalk, eds. *A Handbook of Church Music*. St. Louis: Concordia Publishing House, 1978. Chapters on music and worship, related especially to the Lutheran church.

Harper's Bible Dictionary. Edited by Paul J. Achtemeier. San Francisco: Harper & Row, 1985. A handy one-volume Bible reference, with pronunciation guides for names and unusual words in the Bible.

Hatchett, Marion J. *Sanctifying Life, Time and Space: An Introduction to Liturgical Study*. New York: The Seabury Press, 1976. Liturgical study from an Episcopal perspective.

Hoon, Paul Waitman. *The Integrity of Worship*. Nashville: Abingdon Press, 1971. A systematic, ecumenical perspective written by a Methodist.

Hooper, William L. *Ministry and Musicians*. Nashville: Broadman Press, 1986. A Baptist perspective.

Hustad, Donald P. *Jubilate II: Church Music in Worship and Renewal*.

Carol Stream: Hope Publishing Company, 1993. An update of *Jubilate*, the best overview of the "evangelical tradition," using that designation with its contemporary American meaning.

The Interpreter's Bible. Edited by George Arthur Buttrick. New York: Abingdon Press, 1951-1957. Twelve volumes of articles and commentaries for the entire Bible.

The Interpreter's Dictionary of the Bible. Edited by George Arthur Buttrick. New York: Abingdon Press, 1962. A four-volume encyclopedia that identifies and explains biblical names, terms, and subjects.

Jones, Cheslyn, Geoffrey Wainwright, Edward Yarnold, and Paul Bradshaw, eds. *The Study of Liturgy*. Rev. Ed. Oxford: Oxford University Press, 1992. Essays on liturgy and worship by many different authors, organized by history and topic.

Julian, John. *A Dictionary of Hymnology*. Grand Rapids: Kregel Publications, 1985. A massive dictionary, first published in 1892 and still an extremely valuable resource.

Kavanagh, Aidan. *Elements of Rite: A Handbook of Liturgical Style*. New York: Pueblo Publishing Company, 1982. A pithy and perceptive set of liturgical "rules," "laws," "principles," and "mistakes."

Keifert, Patrick R. *Welcoming the Stranger: A Public Theology of Worship and Evangelism*. Minneapolis: Fortress Press, 1992. One response to our current context.

Lathrop, Gordon W. *Holy Things: A Liturgical Theology*. Minneapolis: Fortress Press, 1993. A fine study of liturgical theology in which the writing matches the liturgy's nonlinear spirit.

———, ed. *Open Questions in Worship*. Minneapolis: Augsburg Fortress, 1994. A set of thoughtful essays.

Vol. 1, *What Are the Essentials in Christian Worship?*

Vol. 2, *What Is "Contemporary" Worship?*
Paul Westermeyer, "What Music Should We Use in Worship?"
Paul Bosch, "Shall We Schedule a Menu of Services?"
Marianne Sawicki, "How Can Christian Worship Be Contemporary?"

Vol. 3, *How Does Worship Evangelize?*
Mark Olson, "What Is Evangelism?"
Frank Senn, "What Is Leadership in Worship and Evangelism?"
Jann Fullenwieder, "How Does the Liturgy Inclusively Share the Christian Faith?"

Vol. 4, *What Is Changing in Baptismal Practice?*
Elaine Ramshaw, "How Does the Church Baptize Infants and Small Children?"
Donald W. Johnson, "How Does the Church Baptize Adults?"
Herbert Anderson, "What Does Baptism Have to Do with the Christian Life?"
Vol. 5, *What Is Changing in Eucharistic Practice?*
James Nieman, "What Is Preaching?"
Joseph Donnella, "What Is Praying at the Table?"
Sarah Henrich, "Who Shall Eat and Drink at the Table?"
Vol. 6, *What Are the Ethical Implications of Worship?*
Stephen Larson, "How Does the Liturgy Serve Justice?"
H. Paul Santmire, "How Does the Liturgy Relate to the Cosmos and Care for the Earth?"
Samuel Torvend, "How Does the Liturgy Serve the Life of the World?"
Vol. 7, *What Does "Multicultural" Worship Look Like?*
Thomas Schattauer, "How Does Worship Relate to the Cultures of North America?
Karen Ward, "What Is Culturally-specific Worship?
Mark Bangert, "How Does One Go About Multicultural Worship?"
Vol. 8, *How Does the Liturgy Speak of God?*
Gail Ramshaw, "How Shall We Refer to God in Sunday Worship?"
Catherine Ziel, "How Do Women and Men Preach?"
Walter Bouman, "In What Name Do We Baptize?"
Lawrence, Joy E., and John A. Ferguson. *A Musician's Guide to Church Music.* New York: The Pilgrim Press, 1981. A practical description for the musician who wants to use his or her abilities in the service of the church.
Leaver, Robin, et al. *Duty and Delight: Routley Remembered.* Carol Stream: Hope Publishing Company, 1985. Essays by a variety of authors on topics related to Erik Routley's life and work.
Lindemann, Herbert F. *The New Mood in Lutheran Worship.* Minneapolis: Augsburg Publishing House, 1971. Brief, easy-to-read, yet thoughtful response to the ferment of an earlier period.
Lovelace, Austin C. *The Anatomy of Hymnody.* Chicago: G. I. A. Publications, Inc., 1982, reprinted from 1965. A look at the syntactic

details of hymns.

Lovelace, Austin C. *The Organist and Hymn Playing*. Carol Stream: Agape, 1981, revised from 1962. A brief, practical description of leading hymns from the organ.

Lovelace, Austin C., and William C. Rice. *Music and Worship in the Church: The Complete Resource for Musician, Minister, and Layperson*, revised and enlarged edition. Nashville: Abingdon Press, 1976. A well-informed, practical manual.

Marty, Martin E. *Baptism*. Philadelphia: Fortress Press, 1962.

———. *The Lord's Supper*. Expanded edition. Minneapolis: Augsburg Fortress, 1997.

———. *The Word*. Philadelphia: Fortress Press, 1984. All three books are brief, easy-to-read, but perceptive introductions to the central topics they address.

McKinnon, James. *Music in Early Christian Literature*. New York: Cambridge University Press, 1987. A very important resource that puts consistent translations about music in the early church together under one cover, with fine introductory comments.

Miller, Patrick D., Jr. *Interpreting the Psalms*. Philadelphia: Fortress Press, 1986. A brief but valuable overview of the psalms, summarizing psalm study in our century and followed by cogent expositions of ten psalms.

The New Interpreter's Bible. Edited by Leander E. Keck. 3 vols. to date. Nashville: Abingdon Press, 1994–. In process. Twelve volumes projected.

Nichols, James Hastings. *Corporate Worship in the Reformed Tradition*. Philadelphia: Fortress Press, 1968. Readable, not overly lengthy insight into the Reformed tradition.

Niebuhr, H. Richard. *Christ and Culture*. New York: Harper & Row, 1951. A classic that delineates five responses of culture to the event of Christ and helps the church musician assess the nature of the tradition he or she serves.

Ochse, Orpha. *The History of the Organ in the United States*. Bloomington: Indiana University Press, 1975. A lengthy and complete historical study.

Ogasapian, John K. *Church Organs: A Guide to Selection and Purchase*. Grand Rapids: Baker Book House, 1983. A relatively brief, but complete overview about various kinds of organs and how to choose one, written in language organ committees can understand.

Pelikan, Jaroslav. *Bach Among the Theologians*. Philadelphia: Fortress Press, 1986. A book-length expansion of the chapter on Bach in *Fools for Christ*, giving a theological context for understanding Bach and his music.

———. *Fools for Christ: Essays on the True, the Good, and the Beautiful.* Philadelphia: Muhlenberg Press, 1955. Studies about value and idolatry as seen through six historical figures, one of whom is J. S. Bach.

Quasten, Johannes. *Music and Worship in Pagan and Christian Antiquity.* Translated by Boniface Ramsey. Washington: National Association of Pastoral Musicians, 1983, first German edition, 1929. A classic study of music in the early church.

Ramshaw, Gail. *God beyond Gender: Feminist Christian God-Language.* Minneapolis: Fortress Press, 1995. A very helpful overview of this matter, with thoughtful opinions.

Reynolds, William J., and Milburn Price. *A Joyful Sound: Christian Hymnody*, 2d ed. New York: Holt, Rinehart and Winston, 1978. A thumbnail sketch of the history of hymnody, with examples.

Riedel, Johannes, ed. *Cantors at the Crossroads*. St. Louis: Concordia Publishing House, 1967. Essays by a number of writers in honor of Walter E. Buszin.

Riedel, Scott R. *Acoustics and the Worship Space*. St. Louis: Concordia, 1986. Why and how to achieve a good acoustical environment for worship, with ample illustrations.

Routley, Erik. *Church Music and the Christian Faith*. Carol Stream: Agape, 1978. Perceptive theological and musical analysis, an update of an earlier volume, *Church Music and Theology*.

———. *An English-Speaking Hymnal Guide*. Collegeville: The Liturgical Press, 1979. Notes on 888 hymns.

———. *The Music of Christian Hymns*. Chicago: G. I. A. Publications, 1981. A history of the music of hymns from plainsong to the present, with examples.

———. *A Panorama of Christian Hymnody*. Collegeville: The Liturgical Press, 1979. Twenty-eight historical vignettes with examples.

Schalk, Carl F. *God's Song in a New Land: Lutheran Hymnals in America*. St. Louis: Concordia Publishing House, 1995. An overview of Lutheran hymnals and chorale books in the United States.

———. *Key Words in Church Music*. St. Louis: Concordia Publishing House, 1978. Extended definitions of concepts, practices, and movements in church music.

———. *Luther on Music: Paradigms of Praise*. St. Louis: Concordia

Publishing House, 1988. A brief but thorough overview of Luther's thoughts about music.

———. *Source Documents in American Lutheran Hymnody.* St. Louis: Concordia Publishing House, 1995. Edited, annotated, and translated prefaces and introductions to hymnals and chorale books in the United States.

Schattauer, Thomas H. "A Clamor for the Contemporary: The Present Challenge for Baptismal Identity and Liturgical Tradition in American Culture." *Cross Accent,* no. 6, July 1995, 3-11. A balanced analysis.

Schultze, Quentin J., et al. *Dancing in the Dark: Youth, Popular Culture, and the Electronic Media.* Grand Rapids: William B. Eerdmans, 1991. A fine, unified series of essays by a group of scholars at Calvin College, which does what they set out to do: make sense of North American society and culture.

Senn, Frank. *Christian Liturgy: Catholic and Evangelical.* Minneapolis: Fortress Press, 1997. A study of the history of Christian liturgy.

———. *Christian Worship in Its Cultural Setting.* Philadelphia: Fortress Press, 1983. The relationship of worship to its culture.

———. *The Witness of the Worshiping Community: Liturgy and the Practice of Evangelism.* New York: Paulist Press, 1993. The relationship of worship to evangelism.

———. " 'Worship Alive': An Analysis and Critique of 'Alternative Worship Services'." *Worship* 69:3 May 1995, 194-224. Historical sources with commentary.

Shepherd, Massey H., Jr. *The Psalms in Christian Worship, A Practical Guide.* Collegeville: The Liturgical Press, 1976. A brief overview of Hebrew poetry, how the church has used the psalms, and the contemporary revival of psalms in worship.

Spurrier, William A. *A Guide to the Christian Faith: An Introduction to Christian Doctrine.* New York: Charles Scribner's Sons, 1952. A description of the Christian faith in nontechnical language.

Thompson, Bard. *A Bibliography of Christian Worship.* Metuchen: The American Theological Association and The Scarecrow Press, Inc., 1989. A massive bibliography.

———. *Liturgies of the Western Church.* Cleveland: The World Publishing Company, 1961. The texts of western liturgies with superb introductions.

Van Loon, Ralph R. and S. Anita Stauffer. *Worship Wordbook: A Practical Guide for Parish Worship.* Minneapolis: Augsburg Fortress, 1995. A dictionary of words and terms related to worship.

Weiser, Artur. *The Psalms.* Philadelphia: The Westminster Press, 1962. Extremely helpful commentaries on the psalms.

Westermeyer, Paul, ed. *Association of Lutheran Church Musicians Parish Education Series: Study Guides Relating to Worship and Music.* St. Louis: MorningStar Music Publishers, 1992.

> Philip Gehring, "The Organ: An Instrument of Worship";
> Carl Schalk, "Psalmody in the Life of the Church";
> Thomas Schattauer, "The Church Year";
> Ralph F. Smith, "Liturgy in the Lutheran Tradition";
> Paul Westermeyer, "Hymnody."

———. "Beyond 'Alternative' and 'Traditional' Worship." *The Christian Century* 109:10 March 18-25, 1992, 300-302.

———. "The Bottom Line: What Provides the Chief Influences in the Direction of Church Music in the Late Twentieth Century?" *Choristers Guild LETTERS* XLVII:5 December 1990, 129-131; reprinted in the *Southern Baptist Church Music Journal* vol. 8, 1991, 22-26.

———. "Chant, Bach, and Popular Culture," *The American Organist* 27:11 November 1993, 34-39.

———, ed. *Meetings House Essays, Acoustics for Liturgy: A Collection of Articles of the Hymn Society in the U. S. and Canada.* Chicago: Liturgy Training Publications, 1991.

———. "The Practical Life of The Church Musician." *The Christian Century* 106:26 September 13-20, 1989, 812-814.

———. "The Present State of Church Music." *Word and World* XII:3 Summer 1992, 214-220.

———. "To Be Human Is to Sing." *The Luther Northwestern Story* 7:1 Winter 1990, 4-8.

———. "Tradition, Liturgy, and the Visitor." *Word and World* XIII:1 Winter 1993, 76-84.

———. "Theology and Music in the Context of Popular Culture." *The American Organist* 28:11 November 1994, 30-36.

———. *With Tongues of Fire: Profiles in 20th-Century Hymn Writing.* St. Louis: Concordia, 1995.

Whale, J. S. *Christian Doctrine.* Cambridge: University Press, 1961.

Eight lectures on central Christian themes.

White, James F. *Introduction to Christian Worship.* Nashville: Abingdon Press, 1990. A standard and excellent ecumenical perspective by a Methodist, revised edition.

―――. *Documents of Christian Worship: Descriptive and Interpretive Sources.* Louisville: Westminster/John Knox Press, 1992. Actual documents that flesh out the previous book.

Willimon, William H. *Word, Water, Wine and Bread: How Worship Has Changed over the Years.* Valley Forge: Judson Press, 1983. Brief historical overview by a Methodist.

Wilson-Dickson, Andrew. *The Story of Christian Music.* Minneapolis: Fortress Press, 1996. A complete overview with many quotations and beautiful pictures.

Winter, Miriam Therese. *Why Sing? Toward a Theology of Catholic Church Music.* Washington, D.C.: The Pastoral Press, 1984. An overview of Catholic church music, Vatican II seen as watershed, and polarities in theory and practice expressed.

Young, Carlton R. *Music of the Heart: John and Charles Wesley on Music and Musicians.* Carol Stream: Hope Publishing Company, 1995. The subtitle gives the contents. With ample quotations.

―――. *My Great Redeemer's Praise: An Introduction to Christian Hymns.* Akron: OSL Publications, 1995. Overview with trenchant opinions about problems that vex us.

Index